Fight Back

Fight Back

81 Ways to Help You Save Money and Protect Yourself from Corporate Trickery

Ellen Roseman

John Wiley & Sons Canada, Ltd.

Library and Archives Canada Cataloguing in Publication Data

Roseman, Ellen, 1947-
    Fight back : 81 Ways to Help You Save Money and Protect Yourself from Corporate Trickery / Ellen Roseman.

Includes index.
Issued also in electronic formats.
ISBN 978-1-11830-088-6

    1. Finance, Personal—Canada.   I. Title.

HG179.R672 2012   332.02400971   C2012-906764-4

ISBN 978-1-118-30148-7 (eBk); 978-1-118-30149-4 (eBk); 978-1-118-30150-0 (eBk)

Production Credits
Cover design: Adrian So
Typesetter: Thomson Digital
Printer: Webcom Inc.

John Wiley & Sons Canada, Ltd.
6045 Freemont Blvd.
Mississauga, Ontario
L5R 4J3

Printed in Canada

1 2 3 4 5 WEB 17 16 15 14 13

To my Toronto Star *editors for giving me the freedom to advocate for consumers; to my readers for giving me their stories and support; and to my family (Edward, Charles and Richard) for giving me the strength to keep up the fight.*

To my literary agent, Brian Wood, for encouraging me to write about fighting back; and to my guest contributors for adding their diverse voices and informed advice to the book.

CONTENTS

FOREWORD

By Dave Chilton

I LOVE ELLEN ROSEMAN'S WRITING.

So much so, I actually pushed her to write the book you're holding. Then I had the nerve to ask to write the foreword (and I normally hate writing forewords!).

Why am I such a big fan of Ellen?

Quite simply because she helps people learn financial planning's most important skill: saving money. Personal-finance educators from Ben Franklin to the Wealthy Barber have preached, "Spend less than you make." Fine advice, indeed. But Ellen takes it a key step further by adding " . . . and here's how."

This book, a truly amazing reference, will teach you how to negotiate better prices and contracts, know your rights (and companies' wrongs!) and make wise spending decisions.

Yes, I sound like an infomercial, but this book will truly pay for itself hundreds of times over. So, act now! Don't delay! Get reading!

And, keep it in a handy place—you'll refer back to it many times. I have already.

Dave Chilton
aka *The Wealthy Barber*

INTRODUCTION

MY FIRST BOOK, *CONSUMER, BEWARE!*, came out in 1974. And guess what? It was defective. The "perfect binding" (actually glue) separated from the pages, causing them to fall out in clumps.

This was embarrassing, as you can imagine. It was also funny to read the letters from unhappy buyers: "I have never written a complaint before, but following the template you gave on page X, I want to ask for my money back."

The publisher, alas, was insolvent and had not paid the binder. But when it was bought by a bigger publisher, I asked the CEO for help. He recalled the books from the stores, rebound them and added a cover that said, "New and improved."

That was my first taste of consumer activism. I succeeded in forcing an unsafe product off the shelves. Meanwhile, the readers who had the courage to complain received a replacement book. Those who did nothing lost out.

As a newspaper columnist, I am attracted to those who shake things up. Even when I veered into financial journalism, I found fertile ground for consumer activism in the mutual fund industry. Many companies treated investment advisers as their customers, while ignoring the needs of investors. That is no longer true.

I spend much of my time trying to help people with problems. There is a double standard in Canada. I call it two-tier service. Most businesses pay little attention to customers after the sale. They cut costs by outsourcing and making you wait on the phone. They send you boilerplate letters that say nothing.

In this book, I give you my best tricks for fighting back in areas where you spend lots of time and money (such as banking, telecommunications, travel and retail). I enlist advice from my best journalistic sources.

Here is my top tip: Your loyalty is valuable. Do not give it away. Tell your service suppliers how long you have been loyal to them. You helped build their brands. You recommended them to others. Without you, they cannot grow as quickly.

Be steadfast. Take nothing for granted. Keep up the fight. When a company says no, take it to the media. Use the courts.

Victory goes to those who are stubborn and persistent. You can get a better deal. You can fight back.

outsmarting the banks

AS CANADIANS, we love the convenience and personal service we get at the big banks. We know our banks did a solid job during the recession and stock market crash in 2008-2009. They withstood the stresses that sunk some financial institutions in the U.S. and overseas. We're proud of their strength and conservative lending practices.

But there are many things we don't like about the big banks. They can make us so annoyed that we head off to smaller financial institutions, hoping to find a more caring attitude and more respect for customers.

Why do banks keep increasing their service charges and adding new charges, despite making billion-dollar profits? Why do they impose fees on products and services we already own without asking for permission or even notifying us?

Suppose you're moving your registered retirement savings plan from one bank to another. You may not see the fees that your bank charges to transfer the investments elsewhere until after doing the paperwork. These fees may not even have existed when you opened your RRSP.

Why do banks play games with interest rates? They often post rates that apply only to customers who don't make an effort to negotiate a better deal. It would be nice if they gave us their best rates right away and didn't force us to grovel.

These fictitious posted rates can come back to haunt you if you make an early exit from a closed mortgage in order to sell or refinance. Banks often calculate the penalty using the higher rate you didn't have to pay, rather than the discounted rate you actually did pay.

Why do banks offer such a dizzying array of credit cards? You can easily get confused, trying to pick the best card for your needs and juggling the competing demands of interest rates, service charges, annual fees, warranties, cash back and travel or merchandise rewards.

Finally, why do banks try so hard to sell you insurance to protect your credit card balance if you get sick or lose your job? They used to do it in a sneaky way, adding it to your account and making you responsible to cancel it. Now the law has changed to outlaw such negative option billing. But some cardholders still say yes to telephone pitches for insurance, not knowing that it pays only the minimum balance each month and costs too much for the benefits that it offers.

It is clear that Canada's big banks can turn off loyal customers with their high-handed behaviour. But they do value your loyalty when you say you are ready to go to a competitor. They do not want to lose you.

You can get a better deal from your bank by playing on this desire to boost market share.

First, you describe what you want and what is available at other banks (after doing some research).

Second, you suggest that you will open new accounts or move accounts from other financial institutions if you get what you want.

Third, you will make an effort to encourage your friends and family to open or move accounts to the bank.

Fourth, you will use social media to talk about your good experience. You will not send negative comments to your Facebook friends and Twitter followers.

You get the picture. Banks want to get a greater share of your wallet. They negotiate with you and make concessions if you promise to send more business their way. They value the influence you have on people in your social and business networks.

If you sit tight and accept what you are offered, you will not get the best deals on products and services. You may only hear about them when you are on the way out the door.

Treat the bank as you would treat a telephone company or car dealer. Do not accept the posted price. Ask for what you want. Keep pushing for more. Explain your worth as a customer. Suggest that you will leave. Then, make the bank beg you to stay.

CHAPTER 1

Get a Higher Interest Rate on Your Savings

THE INTEREST RATES that big banks pay on your savings are rather low. In some cases, they're downright pitiful. So why do many of us keep our extra cash there, instead of moving it to a low-cost competitor that pays a higher interest rate?

I'm talking about the five big banks that dominate the industry: Royal Bank of Canada (RBC), Toronto-Dominion (TD Canada Trust), Canadian Imperial Bank of Commerce (CIBC), Bank of Nova Scotia (Scotiabank) and Bank of Montreal (BMO).

The Big Five have thousands of branches across Canada, which provide personal service, financial advice—and, yes—sales pitches for mutual funds, RRSPs (registered retirement savings plans), TFSAs (tax-free savings accounts) and other lucrative investment products. The cost of keeping branches open and staffed during the week (and often on weekends) forces them to offer lower rates on savings accounts, term deposits and guaranteed investment certificates than virtual banks.

The Big Five just can't compete with smaller banks that do business with customers by phone or Internet. It's much cheaper for rivals to operate without the expense of bricks and mortar. When the Big Five do offer a higher-than-average savings rate, they usually require high minimum balances or punitive fees for transfers or withdrawals.

Look at the book publishing business and how it has changed. You save a few dollars when you buy a book online, even after paying the shipping cost.

You save even more when you buy an electronic book online and download it to your reading device.

Banking has the same issues with higher costs in the real world and lower costs in the virtual world. The Big Five banks have a strategy of offering low posted rates to all their customers and then offering better rates for those who have more value to the bank. They keep their bottom line a secret, so you have to negotiate for the best deal that you can possibly get.

You don't have to settle for peanuts on your savings accounts, term deposits and guaranteed investment certificates. If you're a customer of the big banks, you can do better than the posted rate, as long as you're prepared to shop around and negotiate.

Here's how to get better rates:

- Compare the rates paid at smaller banks compared to those paid by the big banks. You can find a comprehensive list of rates on savings products at the *Toronto Star's* website, www.thestar.com (go to "Business" and then to "Loans and Rates").

- Try Cannex, another comparison shopping site (www.cannex.com). It's aimed at brokers, but does have some free information (such as the rates paid on Canadian deposit accounts).

- If you find a better deal at another big bank or a smaller rival, ask your own bank to match it. Suggest you will walk if you cannot get a matching offer.

- As bargaining chips, talk to the bank about your long-time loyalty as a customer and your family members' loyalty. Talk about the network of people you can influence.

- Argue that if you get what you want, you intend to open new accounts at the bank and transfer existing accounts from other financial institutions. Your network may do the same thing.

- If you suggest that you will take your money elsewhere if you cannot get a decent rate, be prepared to walk away. This cannot be an idle threat, nor can it be delivered in a hostile manner. Your aim is to be friendly, courteous and non-confrontational.

- Decide what to do if your bank refuses to match the savings rates offered by smaller institutions. Will you compromise? What is your bottom line? Will you settle for half a point more than the bank's posted rate? Or will you settle only for a full point?

- Work out your strategy in advance. If you are told that the bank has little room to negotiate on savings rates, ask for a deal on another product. The bank may be keen to sell mortgages and able to help you switch your mortgage from another institution with the appropriate inducements.

CHAPTER 2

How to Fight Back when a Bank Cuts the Interest on Your Savings

CANADA'S BIG BANKS use a two-pronged strategy with savings products. They offer a low posted rate for most customers, but boost the rate for those who have more assets or who negotiate a better deal based on their value to the financial institution. In this way, the banks enhance their profits by market segmentation.

Never assume that you are getting the best rate because you are a long-term, loyal client of the bank. You have to keep asking your bank about savings rates. Never stop bargaining about rates and never stop keeping track of what you are being paid.

Rob Young's story shows what can happen with a bank savings account if you take your eye off the ball. As a TD Canada Trust customer, Young received a letter in 2010, telling him about what appeared to be a minor change. His account (called a Guaranteed Interest Account) was being transformed into an Everyday Savings Account with the same interest rate. He was told that if this account no longer suited his needs, he could book a free assessment at his branch.

Unfortunately, Young did not know that TD Canada Trust was launching a new and better account (called a High Interest Savings Account) at the time. He did not know that he was getting a lower and lower rate on his old account. Nor was he told that he could boost his savings rate by switching, despite many trips into the branch to update his passbook and transfer money between accounts.

Only in 2012 did he learn about the growing gap in interest rates. While his Everyday Savings Account was paying only 0.5 per cent, the new High Interest Savings Account was paying 1.2 per cent. That made quite a difference, considering that he had a $45,000 balance.

"I made about $240 in interest last year, but could have made $540," he said in a letter to TD. "Over the years, I've been asked if I'd like to make an appointment with a TD adviser for mutual funds. But I've never been told about the High Interest Savings Account. Will TD make up the difference since the account's inception?"

Young did not get anywhere with his request for compensation, even though he wrote to the chairman of the board and to the ombudsman. He was told that it was a customer's responsibility to look for other savings opportunities at the bank.

When he wrote to me, I asked if he had other accounts at the bank. Yes, he had a mortgage and he was planning to move his mortgage at renewal time. And yes, he had been a customer for 25 years.

Bingo. I knew I could help him recoup that missing $300 in interest. TD spends millions to show it cares for clients. How could it turn down a request by a long-time client who felt that the bank had tricked him and who was prepared to air his grievances in a public forum?

Luckily, the bank said yes to my request for reimbursement.

"We train our branch and phone staff to have regular conversations with customers to ensure they're in the right account for their needs. We also provide full information about account options on our website (as well as in-branch) and have an account selector tool," said TD spokeswoman Barbara Timmins.

"Unfortunately, the customer did not benefit from either. In this case, we are prepared to make a goodwill gesture to compensate him for the interest rate differential between the two accounts."

Not only Young received an interest bonus. Many other TD customers read my column about the savings account switch and also made a successful appeal for their fair share of interest.

This is another example of the two-pronged strategy used by banks. They launch new products to attract clients or match the competition, while keeping long-term customers in older products that may have fewer benefits. Moreover, they do not tell you about the new products unless you ask.

So, if you miss out on a deal that you think you deserve, always play the loyalty card. Tell the bank that you plan to leave and take your friends and family with you. That can turn the odds in your favour, especially if you talk about your other options and make a credible case for leaving.

Finally, contact the media if you feel you were the victim of a dirty trick. Reporters love stories about corporate wrongdoing. They will be happy to help you tell your tale, as long as you show that you did your best to get the facts. Contacting the media can lead to reimbursement for you and for others caught in the same trap.

CHAPTER 3

Look Beyond the Big Banks for Higher Savings Rates

YOU CAN GET HIGHER SAVINGS RATES by negotiating with your bank and playing the loyalty card. But if bargaining is not your strong suit, there's another option: Hire a deposit broker to do the bargaining for you.

Deposit brokers specialize in finding the best rates on savings products. They have a database of constantly updated rates on different types of products and they can get deals that you cannot get on your own.

Compensation for deposit brokers comes from financial institutions, not from your pocket. They earn commissions from the companies with which they place your deposits. You still get a competitive rate, since the financial institutions treat these commissions as a marketing cost. Thus, your comparison shopping costs you nothing. (Travel agents are compensated in a similar way.)

You may not have heard about deposit brokers before. Do not worry. They have a low profile in Canada. But they are legitimate businesses that have a self-regulatory organization, called the Registered Deposit Brokers Association, www.RDBA.ca. You can search for members in your area and get contact information for the financial institutions with which they do business.

Why do financial institutions deal with deposit brokers? They want to get new business and they want to minimize their advertising costs. Companies such as Concentra Financial in Saskatoon, Bridgewater Bank in Calgary and B2B Trust in Toronto are looking for exposure and use deposit brokers to get their names out to the public.

Deposit brokers often deal with online banks that have few branches or no branches at all. By dealing with customers by telephone or Internet, they can offer higher rates without requiring a high minimum balance.

But there's an important difference between some financial institutions and others. As a customer, you have to ask about deposit insurance. This is designed to protect your savings if the bank goes out of business.

Most of the large banks with branch networks are members of the Canada Deposit Insurance Corporation. This is a federal crown corporation, which was created in 1967 to cover eligible deposits if a financial institution fails. CDIC guarantees deposits for up to $100,000 each. It does not cover foreign currency deposits or those with terms exceeding five years.

You can find out easily which banks belong to CDIC. Go to their website, www.cdic.ca, and click the first box on the home page banner called, "Where are my savings insured by CDIC?" You will see an updated list of member institutions.

With some online banks, you need to know the parent company's name in order to find it at the CDIC's website. For example, Ally Bank is listed under its parent company's name, ResMor Trust Co. Canadian Direct Financial is listed under Canadian Western Bank.

You can find many online banks that offer higher savings rates and that belong to CDIC. They include ING Bank of Canada (soon to be part of Scotiabank), President's Choice Bank, ICICI Bank Canada, Manulife Bank of Canada, Canadian Tire Bank and Peoples Trust Co. This means that they are federally regulated.

You can also find many online banks that are not CDIC members. They are owned by credit unions and they are provincially regulated. This means that your money is protected by a provincial deposit insurance organization. For example, First Ontario Credit Union is a member of the Deposit Insurance Corporation of Ontario (DICO), as is Meridian, Ontario's largest credit union.

However, you have to do your research to find out which institutions are CDIC members and which belong to a provincial deposit insurance organization. Alterna Bank, based in Ottawa, is owned by a credit union and yet it is a CDIC member.

You may find an interesting anomaly while hunting for higher rates. Some of the best deals are from online banks that are owned by Manitoba credit unions. Their names include Achieva Financial, MAXA Financial, Outlook Financial, AcceleRate Financial, Hubert Financial and Steinbach Credit Union.

If you save with an online bank owned by a Manitoba credit union, you are covered by the Deposit Guarantee Corporation of Manitoba (DGCM). Started in 1965, it covers 100 per cent of the deposits held with Manitoba credit unions and *caisses populaires* (compared to CDIC's limited coverage of $100,000 per deposit). It also covers deposits in foreign currencies and those with terms of more than five years (which CDIC does not cover).

DGCM was established under a Manitoba law and its board members are appointed by the province's lieutenant-governor. However, it is not backstopped by the provincial government. The separation occurred in the mid-1980s after a few provincial financial institutions went under. The Manitoba government does not have to provide financial support to DGCM if it runs out of money.

This is different from CDIC, which has legislated protection for deposits. This means that the federal government must step in to cover CDIC if it cannot reimburse all the depositors in failed member institutions. And most provincial governments offer guaranteed support to credit unions in case they cannot cover the failures of member firms.

So, are you at risk when putting money with a Manitoba credit union? This is a question you should consider.

"As the prudential regulator, we make sure that credit unions never get to the point where we have to pay out," said DGCM chief executive Vernon McNeill in an interview in 2011.

DGCM is fully funded according to actuarial guidelines, with reserves equal to about 1 per cent of its insurable deposits, McNeill added. Moreover, there have been no credit union failures in the past 25 years in the province.

Potential customers of Manitoba credit unions are invited to call DGCM's toll-free number (1-800-697-4447). "We answer two to three calls a day about our guarantee," the chief executive told me.

If you are seeking higher rates at online banks, you can find out how your deposits are insured at the website www.HighInterestSavings.ca. You can compare rates at more than a dozen financial institutions and see whether they belong to CDIC or provincial deposit insurance plans.

This website, Canadian High Interest Savings Bank Accounts, has frequently updated rates on both regular accounts and tax-free savings accounts (TFSAs), plus an active discussion forum. It is run by an "interested" volunteer named Peter Keung, who also has a helpful website on prepaid phone plans, www.speakoutwireless.ca.

CHAPTER 4

How to Get Higher Savings Rates without Getting Burned

BEFORE DEPOSITING MONEY with a financial institution, whether you deal with it on the phone, on the Internet or at a bricks-and-mortar branch, you have to ask some questions. Interest rates are not the only factor. You also have to look at transaction costs. You can end up paying more in fees that you earn in interest on your savings.

Here are some questions that you should ask a bank:

- Is there a fee for withdrawals?

- Can you get access to your money any time from an automatic teller machine?

- Do you have to transfer your money from a savings account to a chequing account before you can withdraw it?

- Can you transfer funds to accounts at other financial institutions by Internet or by telephone?

The Financial Consumer Agency of Canada is a federal organization that has a mandate to enforce banking laws and provide information to bank customers. It has a Savings Account Selector Tool at its website, www.fcac.gc.ca, where you can compare rates offered by banks and credit unions across Canada.

You begin by saying how much money you keep in your savings account during a month. Then, you see the rates offered on different balances and you see how the interest is calculated. Is the highest rate applied to the whole balance? Or is a different rate applied to each tier of the balance?

You can compare the features available with each savings account, such as debit card, direct payment, preauthorized debit, cheques and record-keeping options (electronic or paper). Most importantly, you can find out which services are free and which have extra charges.

Some banks have unlimited free transactions. Some banks have limits on free transactions. And some banks charge fees each and every time that you withdraw or transfer money from your savings account and you pay a bill at a branch. The cost can range from 75 cents to $5.

Make sure that you get updated information on fees when opening a savings account. Ask questions, since you may not find what you need in the fine-print terms and conditions. Service charges can wipe out your interest earnings pretty quickly.

Here are other tips from the FCAC on comparing savings account rates:

- Most financial institutions advertise an annual interest rate, but interest is usually calculated daily or monthly. Ask the bank about how often your money earns interest. Each interest payment is added to the principal and also starts to earn interest, a process known as compounding. The more often interest is compounded, the more your account will grow.

- Find out if the financial institution offers a higher interest rate for an introductory period and a lower rate afterward. If so, make sure you know what the lower rate will be, when it kicks in and whether or not it is a competitive rate.

- Your financial institution must provide you with a copy of the account agreement, which lists terms and conditions, plus fees. Ask questions about anything you don't understand. Keep a copy of the account agreement for your records.

- Make sure you understand how the account works. You can run into big problems if you do not read the small print.

You may be surprised to learn that even lawyers do not always read the fine print in their contracts. I once wrote about an Ontario court judge, who found that his bank had frozen him out of his chequing account after he ran an overdraft for six months in a row. He did not know that his agreement had a limit on borrowing through an overdraft.

Things did not improve for the judge. The bank asked him to cover his $2,500 overdraft balance within one day. But he did not want to charge the amount to his credit card and asked for leniency. The bank then froze his account and turned it over to a collection agency.

I think that the judge was not treated with enough respect, given his 25-year history as a customer. The bank could have warned him to pay his overdraft before the deadline. It could have warned about restricting his access to funds if he dallied. But it assumed that he knew the rules.

The rules are a big deal when it comes to Canada's banks. You have to follow them or face the consequences. So, read the agreements you get with your accounts. If you cannot locate them at home, you can usually find them online. And do not run afoul of the requirements.

CHAPTER 5

How to Trim the Bank's Service Charges

YOUR ACCOUNT PACKAGE can cost next to nothing. Many big banks offer free chequing, rebates or discounts to children, students and seniors. And under an agreement with the federal government, many banks offer low-cost account packages to consumers for under $4 a month.

You can also pay as much as $15 to $30 a month for a banking package, depending on the volume and variety of your transactions. That's a substantial amount that you can reduce by doing a little homework. So, start analyzing your banking needs and how to satisfy them at the lowest cost.

Let's look at how to save money on monthly fees:

- Find out if you qualify for free or low-cost banking because of your age. Don't assume you get a discount automatically once you reach 55 or 60. You have to ask about a discount, even though the account documents show your birth date. And even if you ask, you may not get a retroactive refund.

- The same thing applies to children and post-secondary students. They can miss out on discounts unless they make a point of bringing their age and status to the bank's attention.

- Check the low-cost accounts offered by eight banks at the Financial Consumer Agency of Canada's website, www.fcac.gc.ca. (Participating banks are BMO, CIBC, RBC, TD Canada Trust, Scotiabank, HSBC, Laurentian Bank and National Bank.) They allow eight to 15 free debit transactions a month, at least two of which can be made in the branch, as well as free monthly statements or a passbook.

- Some banks that didn't sign the federal agreement also offer customers a choice of free or low-cost accounts. Mid-size banks such as ING and President's Choice have lower fees because they don't have a network of branches to support. Credit unions and *caisses populaires* are also worth investigating.

- Try the FCAC's Banking Package Selector Tool. It's easy to use and shows how much you pay at different financial institutions, depending on your monthly transactions and service needs.

- Before using the FCAC tool, you have to get information about your activity by digging up a few of your recent bank statements. You add up the number of transactions that you do at branches and automated banking machines (ABMs). Then, count the preauthorized payments, bill payments and transfers by phone or Internet and direct payments by debit card that you make.

- You also have to decide which specialized banking services you use on a regular basis, such as overdraft protection, e-mail money transfers, stop payments, personalized cheques and cheque returns.

- Find a package that gives access to ABMs not owned by your own financial institution. Such fees can add up if you withdraw money from other banks three or four times a month.

- Get a list of all the no-fee ABMs in your area. Find a map and print it out. And when you can't get to your own bank's ABM, use the cash-back feature offered by many stores when you pay with a debit card.

Service charges are creeping up again after a long period of stability. You can blame record low interest rates for banks' new focus on wringing more fees from retail customers. So, you have to keep an eye on what you pay each month.

TD Canada Trust raised monthly fees on safety deposit boxes by about 40 per cent in 2012. It was the first of the Big Five banks to eliminate free banking for seniors. (It now offers discounts instead.) TD also started charging $2 monthly fees for customers who wanted to get mailed statements and passbook use.

RBC raised the monthly fee for its Signature No Limit Banking package to $14.95 (from $13.95), but added five free Interac electronic transfers and cross-border debit transactions a month (up from two). It removed monthly bank package fee rebates for seniors who had a Rewards Visa Preferred credit card, but added seven days' out-of-province/country emergency medical coverage.

So, how can you fight back? Here's my advice:

- Read your monthly statements. Are you paying more than before? Find out why. Check the statement inserts to find out if fees are going up.

- Call your bank or visit a branch to ask about cutting your fees. Maybe a new account or plan was introduced since you adopted the one you have. Don't assume the bank will tell you about it. Consider switching to a new account.

- If you don't know about a new service charge until you see it on your monthly statement, ask the bank for leniency. You can usually get a fee reversed after the first month it appears.

- Decide how you feel about electronic record-keeping. Many banks have started charging $1 to $2 a month for paper statements and exempting only those with low incomes, advanced age, health problems (such as poor eyesight) or little access to computers. Find out if you qualify for an exemption. Ask your bank to supply free paper statements for the first year as a loyalty discount.

Think about moving to smaller banks with few or no branches and a minimum of service charges. Talk to friends and family members who have low-fee accounts at smaller financial institutions. Are they happy? Is there anything they miss? How much do they save since they had an account at a big bank? Do they incur extra fees because they go over the limit for monthly transactions?

CHAPTER 6

How to Fight Back when You Miss a Discount You Deserve

THE BIG FIVE BANKS LIKE to offer free banking for students and seniors. But you cannot assume that you will get free banking, even if you are eligible for it. Your student status may be on file. Your birth date may be on file. Still, you may not get free banking unless you ask for it.

You do not have to be 65 to qualify as a senior. The Old Age Security Pension starts at 65, but most banks start offering benefits to those who are turning 60. A few banks lower the threshold to 59.

The question then arises: What if you do not get free banking when you deserve it? Your fees should be adjusted automatically when you reach the age of eligibility, but that is not always the case. When you wake up to the fact that you have lost out on months or years of free banking, you may be too late to make up the difference.

I got an e-mail from a Scotiabank client named Claudine, who did not know about the free chequing account for customers age 59 and up. And by the time that she heard about it, she was already 69 years old. She had lost out on 10 years of benefits.

Claudine was angry because she had renewed her mortgage at age 66. The bank staff could have seen her birth date on her records, but did not mention anything about the free account. She was denied a refund for the free banking she had missed.

The Scotiabank president's office relented and offered to give her back two years' worth of service charges. She felt that was too little and contacted me. The bank then agreed to boost her refund to $300 (double the previous amount), but refused to compensate her for the full decade of charges.

Claudine was happy to see the bank reduce its opposition to a refund. Her case shows that if you keep escalating a complaint to a higher level, you can get something rather than nothing.

Marketplace, a consumer show on CBC TV, ran a story in April 2012 about seniors' discounts at the Big Five Canadian banks. It too noted that rebates were not automatically applied when customers reached the age of eligibility.

Two of the Big Five banks (BMO and RBC) added seniors' discounts automatically. CIBC did not add discounts automatically, but it did give full refunds to those who missed out, *Marketplace* said. Scotiabank and TD Canada Trust were the worst: They failed to add seniors' discounts and failed to pay full refunds to those who missed out.

I often hear from customers who did not get the best deals because they did not ask the right questions. They trusted that company staff would give them the information they needed. Forget it. As Claudine's story shows, you are held to be partially responsible if you do not ask.

"Are there any discounts or money-saving options I can qualify for?" That is a good question to ask your bank every few months. You can also ask: "Is that the best you can do? Can you do any better?"

In March 2012, TD Canada Trust broke ranks with other banks and stopped offering its Plan 60 free account for seniors. It allowed customers to keep free banking if they already had it. But everyone else would get rebates of 25 per cent on three different account packages once they turned 60 years old.

Even that decision was not bound in stone. I heard from many TD Canada Trust customers whose 60th birthday occurred just before the Plan 60 account was eliminated. They wanted to be considered eligible for it because of their long history of loyalty to the bank. And when I handled their protests, most were able to squeak under the wire.

The message to customers is: Do not give up when the bank says no. Keep asking for a discount or free perk that you can get elsewhere. Make it clear that you will switch banks if your business is not valued enough to get a break that others offer.

The same tactic can work if you miss out on a benefit for a few years. Insist on a refund because of your long-term relationship with the bank. Argue that your status should have been updated automatically because your birth date was on file. Also, the staff should have noticed your age when you did some personal business.

Banks will bend the rules for those they consider as good customers. Keep that in mind when you ask for discounts or compensation for missing a discount. If they want to keep you around, they will figure out a way to do so.

CHAPTER 7

Challenge Bank Fees for RRSPs and Other Registered Plans

YOU PUT YOUR MONEY into a Registered Retirement Savings Plan at a bank, but you find that the bank's rates and products are not competitive. You decide to move your RRSP to another bank. Only later do you discover that the transfer costs you $50 or more, plus taxes.

What can you do about these unexpected RRSP transfer fees? First, you can complain to the bank that you are leaving and ask for a refund as a loyal long-time customer. Demonstrate your worth by talking about your other business at the bank that you do not intend to move.

One of my readers decided to fight back when he was charged a $50 "withdrawal fee" (plus $6.50 tax) by TD Canada Trust. His five-year GIC had expired and he wanted to get a higher rate at ING Direct. He was upset by the language that TD used.

"I immediately walked to my branch and raised a fuss. I stated unyieldingly that there were no withdrawals. This was actually a transfer fee or more correctly, a transfer penalty," he said.

"I pointed out that it showed TD Canada Trust to be a sore loser. If I had been warned of this transfer fee, I would never have opened an account with them. Calling this a withdrawal fee makes it appear legal. To mislabel a fee is childish dishonesty. I got my $56.50 back and then transferred the money to ING."

Another option, if your RRSP account is large enough, is to ask the bank that will be receiving the money to give you a refund. It may be happy to cover the transfer-out charges, since it will be getting a stream of RRSP fees from you for years to come.

"Be sure to call and ask for a refund *before* you initiate a transfer," advises the Canadian Capitalist blog (www.canadiancapitalist.com), responding to a reader's question about moving a self-directed RRSP from a full-service broker to a discount broker and being charged a transfer fee of $125. If you are doing this on the phone, write down the name of the agent who agrees to a refund. Do not forget to follow up and call in the refund request once the transfer is complete.

How can you limit your exposure to RRSP transfer fees?

- Consider opening a self-directed RRSP, in which you buy products from other financial institutions and hold them in the same account. You will pay an annual fee, ranging from $50 to $150, to the bank that is administering your self-directed RRSP.

- If you have a self-directed RRSP, tell your bank that you want to pay the annual fee using money held outside the RRSP. This will maximize your long-term savings and make you more aware of the fees (which were not visible before, since they were deducted directly from your RRSP assets).

- Look for a low-cost RRSP account. Most of the big Canadian banks own discount brokerage firms, which tend to waive annual fees on accounts over a certain size. It is common, for example, to charge an administration fee only on self-directed RRSP accounts with a market value of less than $15,000 to $25,000.

- Make sure you know the pros and cons of using a discount broker. While you get lower fees, you do not get any investment advice. You must be comfortable doing your own research and executing transactions online or on the phone without having anyone to offer personal recommendations.

The RRSP is only one type of registered account. You may also have a tax-free savings account (TFSA), registered education savings account (RESP) and registered disability savings plan (RDSP) with the same bank.

Sometimes, your family members—your spouse or your adult children—also have registered accounts with the same bank.

Use your loyalty to demand discounts. Here is how to do it:

- Tell your bank that you recognize the extra work involved in administering registered plans. You have chosen to hold several accounts with the same bank because you value its reputation.

- Mention your concern about the fact that annual RRSP fees can nibble away steadily at your returns. Some banks and brokerages consolidate all the registered accounts held by family members, so that the family will not be charged fees on smaller accounts.

- Ask your bank to add up the value of all accounts you hold—even the non-registered accounts—to see how many assets your family has in its administration. Suggest that you will keep adding to those assets on a regular basis in the future.

- Hint that reducing the annual fees or eliminating them altogether would be a good way to hang on to your business. While you can get special deals by moving your accounts, you choose to remain with the bank as long as it shows some loyalty to you.

Banks compete with each other and with other financial institutions, such as credit unions. They know it is cheaper to keep you as a customer than to replace you with someone new. So, if you offer to keep adding to your accounts and bringing over new customers, they are more likely to give discounts on your RRSP fees.

CHAPTER 8

Watch Out for Foreign Exchange Conversion Fees

BANKS MAKE MONEY when you use your credit card for purchases when you are travelling outside Canada. They also earn money when you use your credit card for purchases priced in U.S. dollars or other currencies, even when you are inside Canada.

Under the credit card agreement, you have to pay the exchange rate when your foreign currency purchase is converted into Canadian dollars *and* a foreign conversion markup (from 1.8 to 2.5 per cent). The markup is not shown separately on your statement, but is bundled into the foreign exchange rate that is applied to the purchase.

Say, for example, that you pay 1,000 euros for a purchase. If the bank uses an exchange rate of 1.42231, your cost in Canadian dollars is $1,422.31. The 2.5 per cent foreign currency fee (or $35.56) is added later, bringing the total cost of the transaction to $1,457.87.

These foreign currency conversion charges have become standard in the credit card industry. There's not much you can do to avoid them. However, you can try to fight back when you make a purchase in a foreign currency and later get a refund from the merchant.

Here is the problem. Since exchange rates fluctuate from day to day, you can end up with less than a full refund when you return a purchase. Peter's story shows the impact of foreign exchange rates when he returned a purchase right away on his CIBC Visa card.

Peter's wife bought an item in Florida, but cancelled the order on the same day when she found that she could not get delivery before she returned to Canada. She lost 6 per cent on the transaction.

The purchase at Pottery Barn Kids cost $70.62 (U.S.). His wife bought the item on April 17, 2012, and paid a conversion rate of 1.027046, bringing the cost to $72.53 in Canadian dollars. She returned the item the same day, but the credit was posted to her Visa account on April 18 (one day later). This time, her conversion rate was 0.962616 and her cost was $67.98 (Canadian).

"Notice that Visa has taken a $4.55 charge for exchange rates in the process," Peter said. "This doesn't agree with the exchange rates posted on the Canadian government's website. Visa is telling me that the U.S. dollar rose by 4 cents in one day, while the government says the difference in exchange rates was 0.11 cents. The exchange rates used in my transaction do not even agree with Visa's own online exchange rate calculator for corporate customers."

It is a mistake to quote foreign exchange rates without factoring in the currency conversion fees added to both sides of the transaction. When using a credit card, you pay an extra 2.5 per cent (as Peter did) when your U.S. purchase is converted to Canadian dollars—and you pay another 2.5 per cent when you get a refund and the cost is converted back to U.S. dollars. That can make a big difference.

Kevin Dove, a CIBC spokesman, said Peter had to absorb the $4.55 loss. A clause in the agreement said the exchange rate "reflects our cost of foreign funds and an administration charge for transaction handling through the credit card network." Another clause said: "Currency conversion may not happen on the day of the transaction."

Juan had a dispute with United Airlines. He paid for three return flights from Toronto to Bangkok and cancelled them within 15 hours, knowing that United allowed penalty-free cancellation within 24 hours.

Although the flights were paid for in Canadian dollars at the airline's Canadian website, his refund came up short by $82.80. United told him to dispute the charge with his credit card company, President's Choice Financial MasterCard. Meanwhile, PC Financial blamed United for sending a refund amount that was less than what he paid. This had gone on for three months.

After I intervened with President's Choice, Juan was offered 81,000 PC points (which would buy $81 in merchandise). He thought that was the end of it. But after I contacted United, he also ended up with a credit of $82.80 in the dispute.

So, what can you do to fight back against foreign currency fees? Here are some suggestions:

- If you travel frequently to the United States, consider getting a U.S. dollar credit card and opening a U.S. dollar bank account. You can save on foreign conversion fees when you pay a U.S. dollar Visa charge using U.S. funds.

- Ask the retailer for help in absorbing a foreign currency loss when you get a refund on the same day or the following day. Say that you will come back again for future purchases and you will tell others to patronize the company.

- Ask the bank for help with the currency loss. Say that you did not understand the implications of getting a refund within a day and you will not make the same mistake again. Perhaps the bank can give you credit card reward points instead of a cash refund.

- Look for a credit card that does not charge foreign currency fees. Chase Cards introduced the Amazon Rewards Card and the Marriott Rewards Premier Visa credit card. Neither penalizes you for purchases made in foreign currencies. Sears Financial has also introduced a card that charges only the exchange rate and not a percentage fee on top of it.

- Check out alternatives to using your credit card when travelling. You can use your debit card and take out local currency from a bank machine. But you may be charged a withdrawal fee to use a bank machine outside Canada—and perhaps a 2.5 per cent foreign currency conversion fee, as well. Check with your bank before travelling.

- If you do use your credit card abroad, do not get taken in by a scam known as dynamic currency conversion. This happens when a merchant offers to quote the final price of your purchase in U.S. dollars, instead of the local currency. "The exchange rate is selected by the merchant and is usually much higher than that of your credit card," says Krystal Yee, a blogger at the *Toronto Star*'s money section. "Make sure you know the currency conversion rates before you buy anything, or download a smart phone app that will do the conversion for you."

CHAPTER 9

Find the Best Credit Cards for Rewards and Benefits

IF YOU PAY OFF your credit card balance every month, you do not care about the interest rate. Instead, you look at the card's rewards and benefits and try to put a value on them. This is not always easy to do.

First, you have to decide what type of rewards you want. Credit cards offer rewards in a few categories:

- **Travel:** You get reward points that can be used for flights, cruises, vacation packages, car rental and other products or services. Sometimes, your travel points can be redeemed for cash.

- **Merchandise:** Your reward points can be used for a variety of consumer goods, which may include groceries, gasoline, electronics, gift cards, vehicle rebates and financial products.

- **Cash back:** You get a rebate, based on a percentage of the amount you spend on purchases and recurring bill payments, that is credited to your account on a regular basis.

Second, what benefits do you want? Credit cards usually offer benefits in a few categories:

- **Travel insurance:** This includes travel medical or accident insurance, trip cancellation or interruption insurance, baggage insurance, flight delay insurance and rental vehicle insurance.

- **Purchase assurance:** You can claim a refund of the cost of the merchandise you buy with the card if it is lost, stolen or damaged in the first few months of ownership.

- **Extended warranty:** You can get coverage for repairs on a product after the manufacturer's warranty expires.

You can find some credit cards that offer decent rewards and benefits with no annual fee. So, you should not consider cards with annual fees unless they offer you better value than a no-fee card.

Here is an example from the Financial Consumer Agency of Canada:

- Eric pays an $85 annual fee for his card and gets 1 per cent cash back on purchases. He never carries a balance.

- Last year, Eric purchased a total of $4,800 using the card (an average of $400 a month). He received $48 (1 per cent of $4,800) in cash-back rewards.

- Eric is paying more in fees ($85) than he is getting in rewards. This card is not worth the cost unless he boosts his annual spending or finds other benefits of the card that he values.

James, however, finds that his credit card is worth the $110 annual fee he pays for it. Here is his story:

- James rents a car for seven days a year. The vehicle rental agency he uses charges $20 a day for a collision damage waiver that protects him against extra costs if the car is in an accident.

- James uses the credit card's benefit and avoids paying $140 for the same benefit provided by the rental agency.

- He saves $30 a year ($140 minus the $110 fee) with this reward. But if he doesn't plan to rent a car next year, he should think about whether the card is still the right one for him.

You can do your own math to figure out which credit cards make sense, based on your annual spending. If you want a shortcut, check out MoneySense's credit card selector tool, which recommends the best credit cards for you among 100 popular cards, www.moneysense.ca.

Suppose you make $500 a month in credit card purchases. You want to know how much you will get in cash-back rewards in a one-year period. Using the MoneySense calculator, you find these results:

- $99.60 back from the no-fee MBNA Smart Cash Platinum Plus MasterCard.

- $82 back from the no-fee Capital One Aspire Cash World MasterCard.

- $60 back from the no-fee CIBC Dividend One MasterCard.

If you have higher spending levels, you can offset a card's annual fee. Using the MoneySense tool to find the best credit cards for someone who wants cash-back rewards and spends $2,000 a month, you find these results:

- $398.40 back from the no-fee MBNA Smart Cash Platinum Plus MasterCard (still the top card).

- $352.50 back from the Capital One Aspire Travel World MasterCard, which has an annual fee of $120.

- $315 back from the Scotia Momentum Visa Infinite card, which has a $99 annual fee.

"Comparing the different rewards systems takes a Ph.D. in physics," said a MoneySense article in July 2011. "As a result, many of us stick with the same old credit cards year in and year out, wondering if there might be a better one out there for us somewhere."

Canadian personal finance bloggers like to analyze which credit cards give the best bang for your buck. Check out their comments before deciding where to apply for your next card.

The Million Dollar Journey blog keeps track of the top cash back cards in Canada that have no annual fee, at www.milliondollarjourney. com. MBNA Smart Cash MasterCard and Capital One Aspire Cash World MasterCard come out ahead, along with three more cards that merit a mention: American Express Costco Platinum Cash Rebate Card, Canadian Tire Cash Advantage MasterCard and CIBC Dividend Visa.

The Million Dollar Journey blogger, who spends $25,000 a year on his credit card, figures that he would get a $394 rebate on the MBNA card and a $375 rebate on the Capital One card. The MBNA card gives bigger cash-back rewards for groceries and gasoline, but the Capital One card has more benefits—such as purchase protection of 120 days (instead of 90 days) and extended warranty for up to two years (instead of one year).

The optimal solution in this case is to combine cards, he concludes, using the MBNA Smart Cash for gas and groceries and the Capital One for everything else: "That would give you 3 per cent cash back on gas/groceries and 1.5 per cent back on all other purchases. Not a bad deal for free credit cards."

As you may have noticed, the Big Five banks don't show up much on these lists. Rather than offer freebies, they charge stiff annual fees for credit cards that offer half-decent rewards.

The BankNerd.ca blog likes the Scotia Momentum Visa Infinite card, which has a $99 annual fee and gives a 4 per cent rebate on gas station and grocery store purchases, plus 2 per cent on drug store purchases and recurring payments. (Both categories have a maximum spending level of $25,000 a year.)

You need to spend only $450 a month on grocery and gas purchases to break even on the Scotia Momentum card's annual fee. BankNerd realized that he did spend $450 a month on grocery and gas purchases, plus $500 a month on recurring bills.

"With my monthly spending, I earn $336 annually through the cash back rewards. This is not a bad trade-off," he said. "If you are the type of person looking to earn cash-back rewards, then this credit card is definitely one you should be considering. In fact, I would go as far as to say that it should be among the top of the list."

Why do bloggers put such emphasis on cash-back cards? The rewards are paid with clockwork consistency and are easy to value. Cash is cash. There's no discrepancy between what you see and what you get.

With merchandise and travel rewards, you have to save a long time to earn enough points to collect them. You may not even get the rewards you want since credit card issuers can—and often do—change the rules in midstream. Rewards points can expire after a certain period of time or can be lost if you're inactive.

The MoneySense credit card tool helps you find the best reward cards for your spending level. You can also check Million Dollar Journey's article on the best rewards cards with no fees.

For travel rewards only, check Reward Canada's ranking of the best travel rewards cards (www.rewardscanada.ca), which picks five cards in five categories each year. There are also excellent comparison charts for the different types of travel rewards cards.

CHAPTER 10

Find the Best Credit Card if You Carry a Balance

THERE ARE SO many credit cards on the Canadian market that it can be hard to make a choice. Each of the big banks has dozens of varieties, with a dizzying array of interest rates, fees, rewards, cash-back and insurance benefits.

If you find yourself overwhelmed, you may simply pick the most convenient credit card. You fill in an application when a promotion arrives in the mail. Or you say yes when someone approaches you with clipboard in hand at a store, asking you to sign up for a new card.

It is important to get the right credit card for your needs. Carrying the wrong credit card can be costly in terms of paying too much interest or getting too few benefits. Why stick with a card that was pushed on you instead of one you really wanted and chose voluntarily?

Start by analyzing your needs. Here is the key question:

- Do you carry a balance from one month to another? How often do you carry a balance and how much is the average amount?

If you cannot pay off what you owe on each bill, you are better off focusing on low rates. Rewards cards are not a good choice for you, since they have high interest rates (18 to 21 per cent, plus possible annual fees). The interest you pay on your monthly balance will probably outweigh the value of the rewards you get.

Most banks offer a choice of cards with low rates (generally about half the rates charged on their premium cards). Some have annual fees as well (in the $25 to $50 range). These low-rate cards are not promoted much, but they are worth checking out if you do not pay in full each month.

- Where can you find the best deals on low-rate credit cards?

MoneySense magazine has a credit card selector at its website, www.moneysense.ca (click "Calculators"). You choose the size of your unpaid balance each month ($500, $3,000 or $5,000) and you get the five best credit cards for your needs. Most important, you see the carrying cost in dollars and cents, including interest and fees.

Suppose you have an average $3,000 balance. MoneySense tells you that Scotialine Visa, which is a line of credit attached to a credit card, has the lowest interest rates at prime plus 1 per cent (secured) and prime plus 4.99 per cent (unsecured).

Here is the annual carrying cost of the five cards on the list:

- $120 a year for Scotialine Visa at 4 per cent.
- $167.50 a year for the TD Emerald Visa at 4.75 per cent (with a $25 annual fee).
- $179.70 for the Capital One SmartLine Platinum MasterCard at 5.99 per cent.
- $299.70 for the MBNA Gold MasterCard at 9.99 per cent.
- $302 for the National Bank Syncro MasterCard at 8.9 per cent (with a $35 annual fee).

You can also try the credit card selector tool at the Financial Consumer Agency of Canada's website, www.fcac.gc.ca. It gives you interest rates for purchases, cash advances and balance transfers on credit cards from up to two dozen financial institutions in the province where you live. It lists the grace period (how long you have to pay before interest kicks in) and each card's rewards and benefits.

The FCAC's tool is great for doing searches when you know exactly what you want. If you are looking for a low-rate card without annual fees in Ontario, you can find 10 that fit the bill. That compares to 64 no-fee credit cards with rates as high as 21.99 per cent.

Low rates are not really low rates if they last only a few months. You have to watch out for traps with teaser rates on newly issued cards and balance transfers from one card to another. Here are questions to ask:

- When does the promotional rate end? What is the regular rate that comes into effect afterward?

- What transactions does the promotional rate apply to? Does the rate apply only to balance transfers and not to purchases? If so, cut up the card and do not take it with you on a shopping trip.

- Can the promotional rate go up for any reason? Some companies will raise your rate if you make one or two late payments in a year or you go over your credit limit.

CHAPTER 11

Watch Out for Credit Card Balance Transfers

PAUL HAD A CIBC VISA CARD with no outstanding balance. He jumped at the chance to transfer a balance from another card to his Visa at 0 per cent interest. He read the fine print and saw that CIBC would charge a one-time balance transfer fee of 1 per cent of the total amount transferred.

When he received his first statement with the balance transfer and the 1 per cent fee, he made a payment well before the due date and for more than the minimum amount. On his second statement, he noticed that he was charged interest just on the amount of the 1 per cent balance transfer fee. He called CIBC's customer service to ask about it.

"The agent said it was their normal practice to charge interest on the 1 per cent balance transfer fee until the entire balance was paid off in full. I asked to speak to a supervisor or manager and was put on hold for a few minutes," Paul said.

"The same agent came back on the line and said that as a goodwill gesture, they would give me the interest charge. But he warned me that if I ever made another balance transfer, I would be forced to pay these charges in the future."

To Paul, it was not a huge amount of money at stake. But his concern was about the principle of charging a balance transfer fee and then charging monthly interest on the balance transfer fee, all under the guise of a 0 interest rate promotion. He felt that the bank's disclosure was not as clear as it should have been.

I suggest that you call the credit card issuer whenever you find a charge that you do not understand and ask a few questions:

- Where is the information disclosed?
- What is the relevant section in the cardholder's agreement?
- How easily can customers understand the disclosure?
- Can customers get a refund the first time they ask about a charge if the disclosure is hard to understand?

Banks tend to bury their mandated disclosure in small print and the type of language that baffles almost anyone without a law degree.

To understand what happened in Paul's case, you have to look at the CIBC Cardholder Agreement (16 pages) and read a section called Application of Payments (page 8).

Here's the relevant section below, which clearly shows what I mean about bafflegab and legalese:

Any payments we receive towards your Credit Card Account are first applied towards your Minimum Payment in the following order:

(a) Interest which has appeared on a monthly statement;

(b) Fees which have appeared on a monthly statement;

(c) Transactions which have appeared on a monthly statement;

(d) Fees which have not appeared on a monthly statement; and

(e) Transactions which have not appeared on a monthly statement.

Your payment will be applied to all items within each of the categories (a) to (e) above in order of interest rate, beginning with the lowest interest rate item(s) within a category and continuing to the highest interest rate item(s) within the category.

The portion of your Balance as set out in your most recent monthly statement that remains after your Minimum Payment has been applied is your "Remaining Billed Balance."

Any amounts in excess of the Minimum Payment are applied when received by us to your Remaining Billed Balance by first dividing your Remaining Billed Balance into different segments with all items with the same interest rate placed in the same segment (for example, all items at your regular interest rate for Purchases would be placed in one segment, all Balance Transfers at the same special low interest rate would be placed in a different segment etc.).

We then allocate your payment to the various segments in the proportion that each segment represents of the Remaining Billed Balance (for example, if Purchases and Cash Advances at the same interest rate represent 80% of your Remaining Billed Balance, 80% of any amount we receive in excess of your Minimum Payment would be allocated to this segment).

If we have received a payment in excess of your Remaining Billed Balance, the excess will be applied to Transactions which have yet to appear on a monthly statement using the same process described in this paragraph for the Remaining Billed Balance.

Banks write their agreements in this dense way to please their lawyers. They know that customers cannot understand the rules, yet they still quote the rules to customers in a dispute. This creates an opportunity for you to fight back.

Make a case that you did not understand the relevant section, such as the application of payments, because of the impenetrable prose in which it was written. Read it aloud to a customer service representative on the phone. Ask if the rep understands it.

Once you have made your point, ask for a refund as a goodwill gesture. Explain that you do not expect to get a refund ever again. You know the rules now and you will not break them.

CHAPTER 12

Watch Out for Expensive Credit Card Insurance

CARRYING A BALANCE on your credit cards can be risky if your life changes. What if you get sick or disabled or lose your job? What if you die suddenly? What if your spouse dies? If you need two incomes to pay the bills, you can get into a financial jam if one income disappears.

Credit card companies sell a product called credit balance insurance that is supposed to protect you in such cases. But it's less appealing than it seems. The insurance policy pays only the minimum amount to keep your credit card in good standing each month if you become sick or disabled or lose your job. It only pays the balance (and only up to a predetermined maximum amount) if you die or become critically ill.

Many people don't know they even have credit balance insurance since it's often sold in a misleading way. Banks used to give it away free for a month or two to new credit card customers. Then, unless you said that you didn't want it, you started paying for it each month when you carried a balance. This practice, called negative option billing, was outlawed by the federal government in 2012 for big banks.

CBC's *Marketplace* did an investigation of credit balance insurance and found that one in four people who had the product didn't know that it was optional and felt that they didn't receive proper disclosure. About one in two thought that the insurance would pay their entire balance if they lost their job or fell ill. They also thought that the insurance policy covered pre-existing health conditions. (It doesn't.)

Credit balance insurance is a confusing product. In many cases, it's not even called insurance. Card issuers refer to it by a variety of short and snappy names, such as:

- Credit Wise

- Account Protector Ultimate

- Credit Protector

- Account balance coverage

- Payment protection

- CardCare

- FutureGuard

Credit balance insurance is usually more expensive than regular forms of life or disability insurance. You may not need it if you are covered by an employer's insurance plans or you have your own life and disability health insurance coverage. You may have income from other sources to cover the minimum payments or a line of credit line you can use to wipe out the balance if you get ill or lose your job.

The monthly premium varies from insurer to insurer, but ranges from 95 cents to $1.50 for a $100 credit balance. This sounds small, but the cost can add up.

For example, if you have a $1,000 balance, you pay 95 cents times 10 = $9.50 a month, or $114 a year. If you're close to your credit limit on your card, the cost of the insurance can push you over the top and make you incur an over-the-limit fee.

The Financial Consumer Agency of Canada (www.fcac.gc.ca) has a comparison chart, which lists the costs and features of several dozen credit balance insurance plans. You should check this carefully before buying. Most plans have age limits, starting at 18 and stopping at 65 or 70, though some cover you until you turn 85. The maximum benefit is as low as $10,000 and goes up to $50,000.

If you get a call from a telemarketer promoting a "balance protector," here are a few questions to ask:

- Is this an insurance plan? What does the insurance cover?

- Which illnesses or disabilities are covered?

- Is a spouse, or the supplementary cardholder if not a spouse, also covered by the insurance?

- When do benefits start after you report an illness or job loss?

- How long are benefits paid?

- Is there a maximum amount of coverage?

- Do you need to have a permanent job to qualify? What if you are an employee with a fixed-term contract?

- Are you covered if you resign from your job?

- If you miss a minimum payment on your credit card, will you be ineligible to receive insurance?

Here are ways to fight back against banks that give you a sales pitch to buy credit balance insurance:

- Just say no. You don't need such high-priced insurance that does so little for you.

- Check to see if you have disability and life insurance as benefits through your job. Both can help pay off your debts if you're ill or you die suddenly.

- If you carry a big balance on your credit cards, your first priority is to reduce the balance. You can do it more quickly if you don't pay monthly insurance premiums.

- Read your credit card statements every month to check for fees you don't understand. Even if it's not called insurance, a giveaway is a small amount that appears regularly on your bills.

- Protest if you have been paying for credit balance insurance without realizing it. Demand proof that you signed for it.

- If you find that you did agree to the insurance after getting a telephone sales pitch, play the loyalty card. Insist that you want to be treated with respect. In return, you will refer friends and family to the bank and move new accounts to the bank.

- If you did *not* agree to the insurance, but simply failed to cancel it after your free coverage ended, use a moral argument. Say that you never consented to making a purchase. Since you didn't know you had it, you didn't look for, or spot, the charges on your bill.

- Ask for a refund of your premiums. Banks cannot currently sell credit balance insurance by negative option billing under the law. Since you were a victim of this discredited sales technique, you deserve to get your money back.

The *Marketplace* investigation found that several of its staffers had credit balance insurance without realizing it. Two of them called their credit card companies to ask for a refund of their premiums. One person, named Jody, got back $1,839.02.

If you want further ammunition when asking for a premium refund, you can mention what happened in Britain. The financial regulator decided that this coverage (called "payment protection insurance") was sold inappropriately by banks and third-party brokers. It fined several big banks and credit card companies, ordering them to compensate millions of customers.

CHAPTER 13

Beware of Penalties when You Break a Closed Mortgage

YOU WILL PAY a penalty to make an early exit from a closed mortgage. This fee can slash your gains if you are selling your house or refinancing at a time when interest rates are falling. The penalty can come as a big surprise if you are not prepared for it. So, read your mortgage contract to see what kind of penalty will be charged if the debt is repaid before the end of the term.

Most open mortgages with variable interest rates do not charge a penalty when you leave. But with closed mortgages, the contract usually specifies that you pay a penalty of either three months' interest or an interest rate differential (IRD), whichever is greater.

If interest rates have been falling, you will pay the IRD. It is there to compensate lenders for the gap between your existing interest rate and the current rate for a term similar to what you have left, multiplied by the number of months left to the end of your term.

The problem with the IRD is the inconsistent way that lenders calculate the penalty. They have a lot of leeway to plug in their own numbers to decide how much money they lose when a closed mortgage is opened up at a time of falling rates. There is no standardization.

Here is a common scenario. You have a 5 per cent mortgage rate, but you find that a 5.5 per cent rate is used in the IRD penalty calculation. You challenge the bank's math and you are told that the posted rate was 5.5 per cent when you took out the mortgage. You were given a discounted rate of 5 per cent, which was available only if you stayed until the end of the term. Since you are leaving early, you have to repay the discount.

Suppose you have 18 months left on your mortgage term. Banks have the discretion to use the current posted rate of their two-year term as a comparison. They can also use the one-year posted rate.

Suppose you have a mortgage that lets you prepay 10 to 20 per cent of the balance each year without incurring a penalty. (Most contracts have this provision.) If you make a prepayment before discharging the mortgage, you can reduce the outstanding balance subject to the IRD. But lenders don't automatically apply your prepayment privileges—and may not advise you to make a prepayment first.

A class action lawsuit launched in 2011 challenges the math used by CIBC Mortgages Inc., a subsidiary of CIBC. It claims that the language was so vague in CIBC's mortgage contracts that the penalties are unenforceable and demands that CIBC gives refunds back to 2005. (You can find information at Siskinds LP's website, www.classaction.ca. The class action is awaiting certification to go ahead.)

Class actions have been used against mortgage lenders before. Several Canadian banks were sued successfully for not including a borrower's prepayment privileges when calculating the IRD penalty. Yet, they still treat prepayments as an option that borrowers must demand.

In 2009, the federal government promised to give more clarity on penalties and suggested that the calculations would be standardized. However, standardization was not part of the reform package unveiled by the Conservatives in early 2012. Instead, the focus was on providing more information to borrowers.

Under a new code of conduct monitored by the Financial Consumer Agency of Canada, banks must disclose penalties in a way "that is clear, simple and not misleading." They must provide prepayment advice on borrowers' annual mortgage statements and supply website calculators to help estimate the penalty that may be charged. They must set up toll-free lines to reach staff members who can give a written statement of prepayment charges if requested.

Banks have to be in full compliance with the code of conduct by November 2012. I like the fact that they will post calculators on their websites to help customers make reasonable estimates of penalties. "No more guess-timators that spit out ballpark penalty quotes that are thousands of dollars off," said mortgage planner Robert McLister, of www.canadianmortgagetrends.com.

Here are some tips to fight back against unreasonable penalties and challenge the bank's calculations:

- Ask about interest rates. Did the bank use the posted rate when you took out your mortgage or the discounted rate that you actually paid when calculating the IRD penalty?

- Ask about prepayment privileges. How much of the outstanding balance can you prepay each year and when? Make the maximum prepayments you are allowed, because they reduce the amount on which the IRD penalty is calculated.

- Ask about portability. Can you take the mortgage with you when selling a home and buying another one? This can be less costly than breaking the mortgage. Can you get a portability period longer than the standard three to four months? How about six months or a year? Your house may take a long time to sell.

- Ask about blend and extend. Can you increase your balance and mortgage term, instead of breaking the mortgage and paying a penalty? Will this strategy work in your favour?

- Ask about the interest rate penalty in three months and six months. If rates fall further, the penalty grows. It is a moving target. A bank can quote a penalty and raise the amount substantially by the time the mortgage is refinanced or the house sale closes. So, act quickly (if you can) to keep the IRD low.

- Find out if you have a mortgage term that exceeds five years. That can be a good thing, since the federal Interest Act prohibits IRD penalties on terms over five years, *after* five years have elapsed. In such cases, a maximum three months' interest penalty may apply.

If you are taking out a mortgage or renewing a mortgage, think twice about using a closed mortgage. Remember that an open mortgage or a variable-rate mortgage will not penalize you for leaving early. You can always lock into a fixed-rate mortgage later if interest rates shoot up.

And if you do opt for a closed mortgage, consider a three-year term. Banks push a five-year term because it is more profitable, but the average mortgage is held only three years. Life is uncertain, so why tie yourself up and pay a big penalty to leave?

Finally, use an accredited mortgage broker to find the best loan for you and minimize the IRD penalty. A skilled mortgage broker can negotiate with banks and help you fight for your rights. They sit on your side of the table, so to speak, when you try to get a problem resolved.

Many mortgage brokers prefer to go to smaller lenders that offer the lowest possible rates and do not negotiate with customers about rates. Smaller banks may have generous prepayment privileges, allowing you to reduce the balance on which the IRD is calculated. (For example, ING Direct allows mortgage prepayments of up to 25 per cent a year, compared to 15 per cent for the big banks.)

Remember that if you break your mortgage, the penalty you pay will be tax-deductible if you move at least 40 kilometres away to get a job, start a business or study full-time at college or university. You report moving expenses on Line 219 of the tax return. Check for details on the Canada Revenue Agency's website, www.cra.gc.ca.

CHAPTER 14

How a Customer Fought Back Against a Bank's Mortgage Penalty

GRACE MODESTO SEPARATED from her husband and sold the family home. She talked to her mortgage lender, ING Direct, and was told that she would not have to pay a penalty if she took out another mortgage within 120 days.

After buying a condominium, she took out a new mortgage with ING. The $7,300 penalty that she paid was supposed to be reimbursed when the deal was done. But she learned that she wouldn't get a refund after all since she had taken out a variable rate mortgage at 2.25 per cent. To get reimbursed, she had to get a fixed rate mortgage as she had before. (The current fixed rate was then 4.5 per cent.)

Modesto argued that she was not properly informed. Peter Aceto, ING's chief executive, agreed that the communication was not up to par after he listened to the recorded phone calls. The message about sticking with a fixed rate mortgage was not made clear to Modesto or her mortgage broker, he said, and refunded her $7,300 penalty.

ING Direct, which tries to be more customer friendly than other banks, relied on both written and verbal disclosure when deciding on this case. At large banks, the emphasis is on written disclosure. When customers complain about their mortgages, they are often blamed for not reading the contract.

Unfortunately, mortgages are written by lawyers in legalese. Without plain language or graphic presentation, they tend to be unclear and hard to understand. Even the bank staff cannot figure out the terms and explain them to clients.

So, keep Modesto's case in mind. Tell the bank that you were not properly informed, since the mortgage was unclear. Try to rule out written disclosure and put the focus on verbal disclosure.

That means you should take notes whenever you speak to bank staff. Keep records of the people you talked to and the comments they made about your mortgage or any other financial issues that are at stake. Read back their remarks to them. Find out if your notes are accurate and if you have captured the meaning. Get staff signatures, if possible, to verify your account of what happened.

In some cases, there will be recordings of your telephone conversations to use as evidence. But only some banks record calls and keep them for a long time. Rarely do you have anything to show what was said when you meet with bank staff at a branch.

So, keep a notebook and pen at hand when you talk to your bank. If you feel comfortable doing it, use a tape recorder on the phone to document what was said. Then, use these notes or recordings as evidence in any disputes about what was said and what was not said.

Banks cannot get away with telling you that you are out of luck because you did not read your contract. Reading the contract does not help unless you are a lawyer or mortgage broker or you are working with a lawyer or mortgage broker. Otherwise, you can make a case that you were not properly informed.

Here is what to say about an important mortgage condition that you did not know about:

- The bank should highlight key clauses by circling them or using large, bold print.
- The bank should contact you before you sign a mortgage to explain key clauses that may affect you.
- The bank should bring key clauses to your attention and ask you to sign or initial them. If you have done so, the bank can assume that you have been informed.

- The bank should encourage you to seek outside help before signing a mortgage, since there is no cooling off period afterward if you change your mind.

Argue that the fault is not yours alone. You are a loyal customer and you expect loyalty in return. You do not accept the bank's argument that you are to blame for not reading the mortgage contract. Instead, the bank is to blame for burying the message.

Remember that your goal is to change the focus of the conversation. You want to make the bank responsible for not giving you the facts that could have helped you make a better decision.

Be diligent, skilled and persistent. Do not take no for an answer. Keep saying that you want the bank to share the blame. This means shouldering some of the costs you incurred as a result of your mistake.

CHAPTER 15

How to Avoid Interest Penalties when Paying Off Your Mortage Early

By Paul Brick

Paul Brick is a mortgage associate at The Very Best Mortgage Company Inc. in Calgary, an affiliate of The Mortgage Centre. He also helps borrowers negotiate with lenders to reduce mortgage penalties at www.mortgagepenalty.com.

HERE ARE TIPS on what to do if you are paying out a mortgage as a result of a property sale (or refinance).

- DON'T assume that your lawyer/notary has reviewed the mortgage payout statement in detail and verified the calculation of the interest penalty. He or she will accept that the lender's information is correct and most times will not question it.

- The lawyer/notary usually requests a mortgage payout statement about 7 to 10 days in advance of the closing. Ask for a copy of the payout statement and have the calculation reviewed independently. Lenders do make mistakes.

- Ask the lender what can be done to reduce the penalty. "If you don't ask, you don't get."

- Consider "porting" the mortgage to the next property (if you are buying a replacement property). Even though interest rates might be lower today, remember that you were satisfied with the rate when you originally placed the mortgage.

- All mortgages have annual prepayment privileges of 10 to 20 per cent. Exercise this privilege prior to paying out the mortgage. This will reduce the penalty accordingly.

- If the sale of the property coincides closely with the anniversary date of the mortgage, consider delaying the closing of the sale until after the anniversary. Then, you can exercise the annual prepayment twice— once before the anniversary and once immediately after. If you have a 20 per cent annual prepayment privilege, this will reduce the interest penalty by 40 per cent. You may have to go to the "Bank of Mom and Dad" to do this, but you can pay any costs they might incur and then take them out for dinner. It will be worth it.

- If you have low equity in the property when selling, consider having the purchaser qualify to assume your existing mortgage. The interest rate may be a little higher than what the purchaser can currently get, *but* he or she will save the default insurance premium from Canada's two major mortgage insurance providers (Canada Mortgage and Housing Corporation and Genworth Financial). There should be no appraisal fee and the legal fees should be lower, as there is no new mortgage to register. The economics at the time will dictate this approach.

- If your mortgage term is six years or longer and you are past the fifth anniversary, the maximum penalty that can be charged by the lender under the Canada Interest Act is three months' interest. (The actual term has to be longer than five years, not just five years plus at the same lender due to mortgage renewals.)

- If you are thinking of selling your property in the near future and your mortgage is maturing, then consider renewing the mortgage on an "open" basis or maybe even on a six-month term.

- Beware of "cash-back" offers when you take out a mortgage. If you sell before the mortgage matures, lenders will want their cash back. Some lenders will pro-rate the amount. Some won't.

- Some lenders will let you pay out the mortgage in full only if the property has been sold. Let's say you get an inheritance or win the lottery. You have to sit there with the cash and do nothing until maturity, unless you sell. You may want to "move on up" and do that in any case.

CHAPTER 16

Why It Pays to Know Your Rights

By Ursula Menke

Ursula Menke is Commissioner of the Financial Consumer Agency of Canada (FCAC), an independent federal government organization that is helping Canadians become better financial decision makers, while ensuring that their rights and interests are respected by the financial institutions with which they do business. Her term ends in December 2012.

IT PAYS TO KNOW what your rights and responsibilities are and how to complain if they are not respected.

you have the right to some free services.

You can cash a Government of Canada cheque for free at any bank, even if you are not a customer, as long as the cheque is for $1,500 or less, and you show acceptable identification.

You have the right to get a copy of your credit report from Equifax and TransUnion, the two main credit bureaus, for free if you order it by mail, fax, telephone or in person, and you must receive it by mail or in person.

you have the right to dispute errors on your credit report.

Protect your credit report by checking carefully for errors and signs of identity theft. You have the right to dispute any information in your credit report that you believe is wrong.

you have the right to refuse some services.

New regulations require that federally regulated financial institutions must obtain your consent before charging you for a new optional product or service, such as optional insurance coverage on a loan or credit card or overdraft protection.

you have the right to faster access to cash from most cheques.

When you deposit a cheque in person with a federally regulated financial institution, you can get the first $100 in cash right away. If the cheque is $100 or less, the financial institution must provide you with the full amount. If the cheque is deposited in an automated bank machine (ABM), the first $100 must be made available the next business day.

Maximum hold periods for most cheques under $1,500 are now four business days if the cheque is deposited in person at a branch, or five business days if it is deposited at an ABM.

you have the right to open a basic bank account.

You can open an account even if you don't have a job, you don't have money to put in the account right away or you have been bankrupt, as long as you have certain required pieces of ID. However, the bank can refuse to open an account for you if it suspects you have committed a crime related to any bank such as fraud, if you harass or threaten a bank employee or if you show false identification.

you have rights when dealing with banks.

As a consumer, many of your rights are protected by laws, regulations and voluntary codes of conduct that the FCAC oversees. When you are dealing with a federally regulated financial institution, you can use the complaint handling process (CHP) of the company if you are not satisfied with the service you have received.

you have the right to dispute preauthorized debit withdrawals.

As a consumer, you have 90 calendar days from the date of withdrawal to report to your financial institution an incorrect or unauthorized preauthorized debit from your account and to seek reimbursement.

you have the right to know how much you would be charged to break your mortgage.

Different mortgage lenders offer different terms and conditions. If you have a closed mortgage, your financial institution may or may not allow you to break it. Before you sign your mortgage agreement, read the information box and the full agreement carefully before signing.

If the financial institution does allow you to break your mortgage agreement, it may charge you a penalty and some fees. If you have to pay a penalty to break your mortgage agreement, your mortgage agreement will describe how the penalty is calculated. It is generally linked to your mortgage interest rate and may cost thousands of dollars.

To find out how your penalty will be calculated, read your mortgage agreement or contact your mortgage lender. Keep in mind that the penalty can change from day to day because it is based on current market interest rates, the outstanding balance left on your mortgage and the amount of time left on the mortgage term. However, the estimated amount that your lender gives you should be close to the penalty.

The FCAC monitors these rights, so if you're having difficulty, visit our website at www.itpaystoknow.gc.ca and have a look at our publications, tools and resources, which are available free of charge. You can also contact the FCAC and we will review the complaint.

CHAPTER 17

How to Outsmart the Banks at Their Own Game

By Matt Goulart

Matt Goulart runs the BankNerd.ca website, billed as "an authority in Canadian banking information."

use your bank's ABMs.

Withdraw money from automatic banking machines at bank branches, so you won't incur fees. Depending on your account, some banks will charge you to withdraw cash by going to a customer service representative.

get mobile banking.

It beats going into a bank branch and waiting in lines. Mobile banking through a smart phone or tablet computer allows you to conduct most, if not all, of your banking needs.

maximize your bank account.

Find an account that has features you use. Additional features usually mean additional costs for features you typically won't use. Don't be swayed by the shiny bells and whistles.

budget accordingly.

Some accounts have a minimum balance requirement, which allows you to save monthly fees. Try to keep that amount on hand all the time and don't get into overdraft.

get your credit card fee waived.

Yes, some banks will waive your yearly fee, depending on how they value you as a client. Don't be afraid to ask. It never hurts.

ask for a lower credit card rate.

You must have a really good credit history to qualify for this. You also need to speak to a supervisor or a manager. Remember to be polite. And if you fail the first time, try again the next month.

tell the bank to remove the hold.

If you've been with a bank for a long time and you make continuous deposits, ask the bank to remove the hold on your account when you deposit a cheque.

negotiate a good mortgage rate.

When getting a mortgage with the help of a mortgage broker, it's important to know that banks can reduce rates. It helps if you are a loyal bank client and you have a close relationship with the mortgage broker. Make sure to send a thank-you gift later to the mortgage broker.

Most importantly: To beat the banks, you must have a relationship with them. Being friendly with a customer service rep will help. Being friendly with a branch manager will help even more. The more relationships you have at the bank or the branch, the better your banking experience will be.

CHAPTER 18

How to Get the Best Service from a Bank

By Douglas Melville

Douglas Melville is Ombudsman and CEO at the Ombudsman for Banking Services and Investments (OBSI). He was appointed in August 2009, after joining OBSI in early 2006 as Senior Deputy Ombudsman for Banking Services.

shop the banks, the bank alternatives and the person you want to bank with.

You have the most leverage in your banking relationship when you are looking to establish a new relationship or are openly considering changing to another one. Use that leverage. Find a person you are comfortable with, someone who understands your needs and can provide the type of banking service and advice you see as valuable.

Canada has a variety of banks, credit unions, *caisses populaires* and trust companies that can provide for your banking needs. Shop those options.

Keep in mind that with all the electronic banking options available in the market, you are not necessarily bound to the bank that is located close to you. Consider other options if you do not require in-person service very often or at all. Sometimes you may wish to obtain some of your required banking services from different providers to get the best that each has to offer.

take the time to choose the right account(s) and product(s) for you.

There are many banking options out there, including perks, loyalty benefits and fee waivers with minimum balances. It can all be very confusing. This makes finding a good banker even more important.

Take the time to understand and consider the options. Read and understand the application forms you are signing and know what obligations you are agreeing to. Seek out advice if you are not sure about something.

carefully manage your account.

Bankers don't like unauthorized overdrafts or bounced cheques. Such problems indicate you are not taking good care of your finances. This makes bankers nervous. It also triggers big fees.

Embrace technology. Online banking can provide you with balance or transaction alerts. Arrange direct deposits wherever possible and set up automatic transfers to make sure the money needed is in the correct account on the day it is needed. Keep track of your finances. Make a budget so you are aware of what you make and spend.

don't make it easy for the bad guys.

Check your statements. It helps you spot errors, which are very rare, but they can happen. It can help spot fraud on your accounts. Credit card fraud and debit card fraud are still significant problems in our society.

Make sure that all the transactions on your statements are yours. Report any transactions that were not made by you. When you no longer need your statements, shred them. Your banking documents contain lots of useful information that could allow someone to open other accounts in your name. Don't just throw all that personal information into the trash or recycling. Shred it first.

Check your credit bureau records periodically (you are entitled to one free report each year) to make sure that your file is in good order. If you see activity on your credit bureau file that makes no sense to you, ask about it.

It could be an old account you no longer use—or it could be someone opening an account in your name.

don't be afraid to ask for help.

If you see tight financial times ahead, it is best to speak with your banker before trouble hits. This way, the banker is prepared and can often assist in some way to help you get over a rough period. If you wait until trouble hits, it can be a lot more difficult getting the help you need.

There are services in the community to help when you get into financial difficulty (such as credit counselling agencies). Know your options. There is also lots of good information available over the Internet comparing options and offering good advice on things to consider in managing your personal finances.

know you have the right to complain.

Give your banker the chance to make it right when you have a complaint. If they cannot or will not make it right, then escalate your complaint. Canada's banks are all required to have an internal complaint handling process and are required to be a part of an external independent complaint handling process like the Ombudsman for Banking Services and Investments (OBSI), which can review your complaint for free if you are unable to resolve it with your bank.

CHAPTER 19

How to Get the Best Service from a Bank if You Own a Business

By Douglas Melville

have a great business plan.

Nothing creates a better start to a banking relationship than a great, well-thought-out business plan. Use available books, online resources and community support resources for small business to help you build on a great idea and create a viable business plan.

have your banker visit your place of business.

One of the best ways to put a banker at ease is to invite them to personally see a well-run operation. Bankers like to check your commitment of time and money. If they are considering lending you money, bankers always want to see that you have a big stake in your business as well.

share your plans and ideas.

Bankers like to hear these thoughts about the future because it often opens doors for them.

You think you may need more space. Your banker sees an opportunity to provide a commercial mortgage.

You are considering expanding. Your banker sees the possibility of offering equipment loans or leasehold improvement loans.

You succeeded in landing a huge, high quality account. Your banker sees an opportunity to provide an increased operating line of credit.

A good banking relationship is a partnership. You can always shop for your financial needs if you wish, but having your banker know what they might be can create good options and gives your banker a chance to earn your business loyalty.

have a backup plan.

While bankers like good news, you know your banker will also ask, "What if something goes wrong?" As with your personal banking matters, the worst thing you can do is surprise your banker with bad news. Before the question is even asked, provide your backup plan in case the pieces don't fall into place as you expect. This will provide the banker with a level of comfort that will be valuable if new financing is being considered.

don't put all your eggs in one basket.

While having all of your business with one banker can give you valuable leverage and access to package pricing opportunities, there are sometimes good reasons for spreading your business around a bit.

If you keep your operating account with the same bank where your loans are, your funds could be seized by the bank if you get behind on your loan. This is when the bank uses something called a "right of set-off." Having some funds that are beyond the reach of your lending bank could provide you a little extra room to breathe if you experience financial difficulties. This same principle applies to your personal banking.

know you have the right to complain.

Give your banker the chance to make it right when you have a complaint. If they cannot or will not make it right, then escalate your complaint. Canada's banks are all required to have an internal complaint handling process and are required to be a part of an external independent complaint handling process like the Ombudsman for Banking Services and Investments (OBSI) which can review your complaint for free if you are unable to resolve it with your bank.

PART 2

keeping your finances on track

YOU THINK THAT you are doing a good job managing your money. Then, you are turned down when you apply for a loan or a new credit card. What happened? You make inquiries and find that there is a problem with your credit report.

It is important to check your credit report on a regular basis. You have to contact Canada's two credit bureaus, Equifax and TransUnion, and ask for a free copy. Then, you have to check your credit report to see if there are any errors or omissions.

There are many reasons why you may have to update a credit report:

- You may find a debt that you paid off shows as being unpaid.

- You may find a bill that you felt was unjustified shows as an unpaid debt. You want to add a note saying that it is disputed.

- You may find that you have been mixed up with someone else, even if the names are dissimilar.

- You may find an item on your credit history that does not belong to you. Perhaps it should be on someone else's report.

- You may find that you have been reported as deceased, when you are alive and kicking.

It can be a challenge getting mistakes corrected, since credit bureaus are not always easy to reach. You have to gather your payment records and get ready to argue your case. But it is worthwhile to straighten out your credit report, as you will see in this chapter.

Once you have your finances under control, you can start to save and invest for the future. The question then is, should you handle your own investments, or use a financial adviser?

Do-it-yourself investing is easier than ever. You can open an account at an online brokerage, pick your own securities and learn how to trade. There is a wealth of information online. But you need time to review your investment choices and the ongoing health of your portfolio.

On the other hand, you may not want to be bothered. You are too busy to follow the stock markets and make difficult decisions on what to buy and sell. Perhaps you feel intimidated. You did not study economics and you find the business news quite mystifying. So, you look for financial advice from a bank or an investment dealer. You ask friends and family for referrals. You interview a few people and hand over your hard-earned savings to someone who seems honest and reliable. You hope that the adviser will put your interests ahead of his or her own interests.

The partnership can prosper for years if you keep close contact with the person handling your investments and you see your money growing. But sometimes, you find that your savings shrink and your adviser does not call or communicate with you. Then, it is time for a divorce and a fight over the spoils. You will find tips on getting redress in this chapter.

Another aspect of getting your finances under control is paying the right amount of tax and no more. Income taxes make up a huge proportion of your lifetime expenditures. Why give the government more than its rightful share?

There are a few legal ways to pay less tax, but you can get into trouble if you do not follow the rules. Then, you start getting letters from the Canada Revenue Agency to pay taxes owing. The interest keeps rising and penalties may be added, as well.

Many people ran afoul of the rules when they put money into a new product, the tax-free savings account (TFSA), which came out in 2009. They knew about the $5,000 limit on annual contributions to a TFSA, but did not realize that any money removed and replaced in the same calendar year would be counted as an over-contribution.

The Canada Revenue Agency sent out many demands for taxes owing, creating fear among those who received them. The tax penalties for over-contributions far exceeded any income earned on the TFSA. However, most people who wrote to the CRA to ask for leniency did receive refunds. Some asked their advisers to write to the CRA, too.

You can go to the Office of the Taxpayers' Ombudsman if you feel that you have been treated unfairly by the Canada Revenue Agency. In this chapter, you will find tips from the ombudsman, J. Paul Dubé, on how to fight back against the CRA.

CHAPTER 20

How to Check on Your Credit Report and Credit Score

YOUR CREDITORS are talking about you behind your back. They keep track of the times when you paid your bills after the due date and the times when you left your bills unpaid. They update your payment history at Equifax and TransUnion, Canada's two credit bureaus, for the benefit of other creditors who may want to do business with you.

You should be participating in these ongoing conversations. But you can do so only by contacting the credit bureaus and asking for a free copy of your credit report. You are entitled to get one under the law.

Many readers tell me that a credit report costs money ($15 or so). That is the amount charged by the credit bureaus, www.equifax.ca and www.transunion.ca, for instant access online. But you can still order a free credit report to be sent to you by Canada Post.

Once you get a copy, you can look for inaccurate data that should be removed or changed. You can call your credit granters to ask them to update the credit bureaus on your status. Or can you can go directly to the credit bureaus to check with your credit granters and make the necessary corrections.

The credit report shows your interaction over the years with companies that give loans, lines of credit and credit cards. It shows your ability to pay bills promptly and any black marks on your credit, such as a personal bankruptcy, consumer proposal or debt management plan done through a credit counselling agency.

Your credit report shows your payment history. It is not the same thing as your credit score, which costs money to check (about $10 to $20). You do not have the legal right to get a free credit score.

The Financial Consumer Agency of Canada explains the difference between the two products in an excellent guide, *Understanding Your Credit Report and Credit Score*, and in a quiz at its website, www.fcac.gc.ca.

Here are some tips on understanding your credit score:

- It is a three-digit number that indicates the risk you represent for lenders, compared to other consumers.

- Equifax is licensed to use the credit score developed by Fair Isaac & Co. (FICO), known as the Beacon score in Canada. TransUnion uses a slightly different score (called Empirica).

- Both credit bureaus use a scale of 300 to 900. The higher the score, the lower your risk to the lender.

- Lenders often have their own ways of arriving at credit scores. They use your score to set the interest rate you will pay on loans and mortgages, known as risk-based pricing.

- The formulas (or algorithms) used to calculate a credit score are highly secret. You do not get a detailed explanation of your score, but you do get a few general rules.

- It is hard to fight back when you suspect that your credit score is not accurate. But you can try to improve it by making adjustments to your outstanding accounts and balances.

So, what influences your credit score? Eric Putnam helps people improve their credit scores though his company, Debt Coach Canada. He offered me his own interpretation:

- The biggest part of the score (35 per cent) is your payment history. This shows if you pay bills on time, have any unpaid debts or have been through bankruptcies, consumer proposals or debt management plans.

- Another big part (30 per cent) is based on how much you owe. If you carry an $8,000 balance on a credit card with a $10,000 limit—even if you pay the minimum amount on time each month—your credit score will drop.

- Another 15 per cent is based on how long your accounts have been open and used. To be seen as a good credit risk, it is not enough to be approved for credit. You have to use the credit that you are given.

- Another 10 per cent depends on the amount you have in revolving credit (such as credit cards) and instalment loans (such as mortgages). Lenders like to see both types of credit. Revolving credit can be maxed out since the rates are high enough to absorb losses, while instalment loans with fixed payments must be approved and supervised closely.

- The remaining 10 per cent is based on how much new credit you have obtained or applied for. This should not be too high a percentage of all the credit shown on your file.

- Check for old credit cards that remain on your file, even if you cancelled them. Having too much available credit can hurt your credit score. Lenders may worry that you have the ability to spend more than you can possibly pay back.

- Take care when closing accounts, since that can also hurt your credit score.

- Suppose that you have three credit cards with available credit of $20,000. Your balances stay under $6,000, which means that you use less than a third of your credit. If you cancel one card with a zero balance and a $10,000 limit, you will be using 60 per cent of your available credit and your credit score will drop.

- Do not make too many credit applications. Having several lenders asking about your credit at the same time can indicate that you are desperate for financing.

- Your credit score does not change when you ask for information about your own credit report. So, feel free to check your report once a year.

CHAPTER 21

How to Correct Errors on Your Credit Report

By Ross Taylor

Ross Taylor is a fee-based financial adviser in Toronto, who is a debt and credit specialist, as well as a licensed mortgage agent. He loves helping regular people solve their financial problems. Visit his website, www.askross.ca.

YOU APPLY FOR A LOAN or credit card, job or apartment, but find that you have a problem with your credit report. The vast majority of errors can be removed. The issue is how to clean up your credit report as quickly as possible. You can use one of three basic approaches:

1. Explain it all to the new creditor and have them contact the bureau directly. Many bankers and loan officers can do this. Certain errors can be cleared up this way—for example, identification issues or items showing as unpaid, when you can clearly show evidence to the contrary.

2. Contact the concerned creditor. Persist until you find someone who will take ownership of the problem and contact the bureau to clear the error. This works well when an item is showing as unpaid or a bad debt, but in fact the matter has actually been settled.

3. Deal with the credit bureaus yourself. This is time consuming. It usually takes up to four weeks (if all goes well). Chances are that if your Equifax report shows an error, the error will show up on your TransUnion Canada report too. Be sure you deal with both bureaus concurrently. Creditors may deal with either or both and you won't know which.

Here are some additional tips on dealing with Canada's two credit bureaus:

- When you initiate an investigation with Equifax, you are expected to have a current report at hand, one that clearly identifies the error.

- When I do this, I deal with TransUnion concurrently and cite the error in the Equifax report. But I don't need to actually order a TransUnion report to initiate the process with them.

- Don't waste your time calling the credit bureaus. They will never resolve a dispute that way. Faxing is best. To be safe, send a package by snail mail, too, to "Account Maintenance." Fax to Equifax at 1-514-355-8502. Fax to TransUnion Canada at 1-905-527-0401. Their mailing addresses are easily found on their websites.

- Try to get their attention and stand out from the crowd. Since they will receive hundreds of other letters that day, plaster something along the top and bottom of the page, such as:

  URGENT MATTER PLEASE—MORTGAGE APPROVAL PENDING.

- Provide two, ideally three, pieces of identification that show who you are and where you live. Copy the front *and* back. At least one should be photo ID (but not a provincial medicare card). Your social insurance card is the best second piece of ID. The third can be a credit card statement or a utility bill.

- Make sure the copies are clear and legible. Copying and faxing can often degrade the legibility of what you are sending. Take extra care with this step. You might end up waiting three weeks just to get a letter saying they could not proceed without confirming your ID.

- Include a clear and concise statement of the issue and why you think it should be addressed. Provide copies of all relevant documents. A summary of notes taken during various calls and other steps already tried can be helpful. The credit bureau will initiate an investigation and write back within a few weeks, enclosing a copy of your current report. Their letters are often cryptic and it is not clear that they have actually done anything. But the new credit report will tell you if the matter has been resolved. If you don't like the resolution, persist.

- No matter how cooperative people seem to be on the phone, once you hang up they are on to the next file. The only person really affected by this problem is you, so follow through!

- Take good notes of your conversations. Keep asking to speak to other people until you find the right person to either resolve the matter or escalate it on your behalf. Whenever someone offers to take a positive step, document it and follow up religiously. Don't give up because you seem to be getting the runaround.

- Keep a file folder on the subject with any relevant notes, documents, statements and reports.

- If you are not satisfied with a creditor's response, find out if there is an ombudsman for their business (insurance, banking, etc.) who can get things done. Just ask and you will be given the ombudsman's contact information.

- Order a copy of your credit report at least once a year. The easiest-to-read versions can be ordered online and include your score. You can do it more frequently if you are correcting a problem or if you plan on obtaining credit, applying for employment or renting an apartment.

- Don't bother subscribing to a monthly credit watch service at $14.95 per month (or more). While it is true that your credit history is constantly changing, 99 per cent of the changes are routine. Constant monitoring is excessive—once or twice a year is enough—especially if you pay attention to your bills and statements.

CHAPTER 22

How to Fight Back when Your Credit History Is a Mess

By Ross Taylor

YOU ENVY YOUR NEIGHBOUR who scored a 0.9 per cent lease rate on her new car. Your sister boasts of her 2.99 per cent fixed rate mortgage for five years. And you fear that your next employer will not hire you because your credit history sucks.

You live in a world of 29.9 per cent used car loans and private second mortgages at 13 per cent. You cannot rely on a credit card to pay for travel. Even making an exit from a paid parking lot poses challenges without a credit card.

Somewhere along the way, you messed up your credit history and you never got around to fixing it. You just began to accept the inconvenience as a cost of living and you developed ways to work around it. But it eats you up. It's time to take back your credit history and fight for what everyone else has.

First thing you have to do is see what credit grantors see when they check your credit history. Access a copy of your report today—refer to earlier in this section if you missed how to do it.

Read and understand each item in your report. In addition to your basic personal information, your report will highlight four key areas:

1. The loans and credit facilities from your past and present and your repayment history with each. Each late payment will be there in painful detail—and whether or not you were 30, 60, 90 or more than 120 days late.

2. The extent to which you use these credit facilities. The closer your balances are to their limits, the less attractive you look.

3. Inquiries by third parties. When you seek credit, sign a cellphone contract, open a new bank account or securities account, for example, you allow these companies to access a copy of your credit report. Generally speaking, lots of inquiries are a warning sign to credit grantors. As time passes, their impact on your score wanes. And in fact, most disappear after three years.

4. There is also a public records section that deals with trouble items such as unpaid collections, written-off debts, bankruptcies, consumer proposals and child support arrears.

I have seen some very ugly credit reports in my time, but it is never too late to begin the repair process. Annotate your printed report for key milestone dates along the path back toward an excellent credit rating.

- In most provinces, six years is how long it takes for the majority of derogatory items to be removed from your credit report. Time will be your friend in this regard.

- Check the dates of your late payments or the date of the last activity on a bad debt or collection. Add six years to that date and note when the item should fall off your report.

- Some derogatory items should not be ignored. For example, some collection agencies wait until six years have almost passed and then restart the process, so you are at risk of waiting another six years.

Don't make the mistake of focusing on problem elimination alone. You also need to generate fresh, positive information with new credit and loan facilities. Otherwise, in six years you could end up with no credit score at all.

- To rebuild your score, ask your bank for a credit card that is secured by a deposit of your own money. If you regularly deposit your salary there and pay bills from their account, they should agree to this. The credit limit can be as little as $500 to get started.

- You can apply for a secured credit card within a few months of starting a consumer proposal or after completing a personal bankruptcy.

- As soon as you can, arrange a second secured credit card. Ideally, this will be from another major bank, but if not, you can always ask Capital One (www.capitalone.ca) or Home Trust (www.hometrust.ca) for one.

- Any new instalment loan serviced properly by you will help rebuild your score. Some people take out a loan, even though they don't need one, and then pay it off early.

- One or two years hence, although there may still be some ugly information on your credit report, you will already have taken huge steps towards rebuilding your score—it will have improved dramatically since day one—and that's just the beginning. As the old bad stuff falls off, your picture gets brighter and brighter.

Some people resign themselves to having bad credit. They wear it like a badge of dishonour and they never get around to fixing it. Though it takes a little work, the financial and emotional benefits of putting this house in order are well worth it.

CHAPTER 23

How to Make Sure Your Credit History Stays Healthy

By Ross Taylor

EVEN IF YOU ARE RISK-AVERSE and don't believe in borrowing money, your life will be smoother if you build and maintain an excellent credit rating. All you have to do is demonstrate that you have accessed and used available credit or loans in a responsible manner.

Here's how to avoid having really bad stuff showing up in your credit report:

- Get a fresh copy of your report once or twice a year.

  That helps you nip some potential problems in the bud. Someone may have been using your identity fraudulently, or a creditor may say that you made late payments and you don't agree with that assessment.

- Do not co-sign for someone else's mortgage, loan, lease or even cellphone contract.

  You have no idea how and if he or she will pay their bills. Whenever you co-sign, you are effectively handing over your credit history to that person.

- Don't ever make late payments.

  Creditors don't care if you moved, went on holiday or had the dog chew your mail. Even when money is very tight, you should find a way to make a minimum payment. But if you are late, it may be OK, since a payment that is within 30 days of the due date will not actually register as a late payment on your credit report.

- If you fall behind on a payment, be sure to make up *that* missed payment as soon as possible.

  Some people simply remain one payment behind for the rest of the term of the loan. They are shocked to find out later that this actually registered as 18 different late payments on their credit report.

- If you wish to dispute a charge on your credit card, pay the amount up front and trust the credit card company to reimburse you when the truth comes out.

  I have seen many people indignantly refuse to pay. In the meantime, their card goes into late payment status and their credit report takes a beating.

- Don't trash your statements without checking them first, even if you never use the card.

  This way, you will notice unauthorized card usage right away. It also prevents an accident when the card company bills you automatically for your annual fee.

- Don't ignore a matter that has led to a collection.

  Settle it promptly—you may even be able to negotiate away penalties and interest charges. At least the item will show as paid or settled in your credit report. Yes, it's a bruise, but it is not a catastrophe.

  Finally, if you want a really strong credit score, try to avoid creditor inquiries at all costs and pay your balance in full each month. Only use your card when you know you have the money to pay the balance in full. I don't wait for my due date. I pay off my credit cards every week or two online.

CHAPTER 24

How to Fight Back Against Bad Financial Advice

YOU HAVE MONEY to invest for the future and you want to get advice. How much do you need to save to reach the goals you have in mind? What investments are suitable for you? How much risk can you handle? Will your money last as long as you do in retirement? How safe is your company pension?

Such questions are hard to address on your own. But many advisers are eager to give you some answers. Armed with financial planning tools, they will put together a scenario that shows you need to save more and earn a higher investment return. Life insurance is often part of the mix.

When you meet with an adviser offering product recommendations, you have to try to figure out if you are dealing with a true professional or a salesperson. Here are some questions to ask:

- Are you registered? With whom? Then, double-check the registration on your own. Clients of Earl Jones in Montreal were shocked when he went to jail for running a $50 million fraudulent Ponzi scheme. He was not registered with a securities commission, which meant that his finances were not audited.

- What training do you have? What are the initials after your name and how do they help me? What continuing education courses are you taking?

- Do you have any financial planning credentials or designations? Look for a CFP (certified financial planner), who has taken a variety of courses over several years and has to prepare an actual financial plan to pass the final stage.

- Can I see a plan prepared for someone else?

- How are you paid? Do you earn commissions from product sales? Do you charge a fee based on an hourly rate or a percentage of the assets you manage?

- What products are you licensed to sell?

- Can I see any testimonials from your clients? Can I call them and ask them about you?

You should do an online search to turn up any dirt on advisers and their employers. Look for disciplinary proceedings or reprimands from securities regulators. Check the number of complaints about the firm in the latest annual report by the Ombudsman for Banking Services and Investments (OBSI), www.obsi.ca.

Once you start working with an adviser, even someone who sells mutual funds at a bank, you have to fill out an account application. Take your time doing the paperwork. Do not let the adviser write down any information on your behalf.

The account application is more important than you realize. It can be a crucial piece of evidence if you complain that the adviser sold you investments that turned out to be too risky for you. The first question will be, "What does it say on the form?"

Also called the "know-your-client" (KYC) form, the account application requires you to check off a series of boxes. How much knowledge do you have about investments? How much experience do you have? What are your goals? How much risk can you handle?

A reader named Joy told me that her adviser was moving from one firm to another and gave her some papers to sign. "Just a formality," he said. Before sending them, she wanted to get my opinion first.

I looked at the account application and realized that he had checked off the boxes in a way that gave him the freedom to invest her money any way he liked. Investment knowledge? High. Investment experience? High. Tolerance for risk? High. Goals? One hundred per cent growth.

Joy was not a person who would give these answers. She was over 65 and had little investment knowledge or experience. A novelist who lived on her investment income, she did not want any growth, let alone 100 per cent growth. Growth is used as a euphemism for highly volatile and more risky investments.

Why was the account application so inaccurate? I could only conclude that the adviser wanted to sell anything to Joy and protect himself from disputes about suitability. If she complained, he could say that she was a sophisticated client with a high risk tolerance. Joy could deny it, but would have to explain why the paperwork confirmed his view.

So, here is my advice about what to do when presented with an account application form:

- Tell the adviser that you want to do it yourself at home.

- Do not check off any boxes if you are not sure what they mean. Ask questions first and then fill out the form.

- Ask your adviser to sign it and give you a copy. Keep it in a place where you can refer to it in the future. Do not lose it.

- Review and update the form at regular intervals. You may want to change your risk level and investment objectives as you get older and your income changes.

- Never sign any papers presented to you as a formality. Watch out for unethical behaviour by an investment adviser.

- If you find out that changes were made without your knowledge or permission, fire the adviser. Joy did so and found someone else who was more ethical.

CHAPTER 25

How to Make Sure You Have the Right Investments

By Douglas Melville

find a good financial adviser and meet with him or her periodically.

There is a difference between a true financial adviser and someone who is merely selling you securities. Know the difference and be clear about what you want and expect from the person.

Finding someone you have confidence in and with whom you can work comfortably is very important. Ask him or her about his or her training, experience and approach to investing and working with clients. Check with securities regulators to see if she or he has had any regulatory violations or any pending complaints.

Your financial adviser is responsible for knowing your financial circumstances and understanding your financial needs and objectives, risk tolerance and level of familiarity with investments, so that he or she can make suitable investment recommendations for you. Come prepared to each meeting. Ask questions and keep notes. Maintain a written record. Keep your financial adviser advised of changes in your life (job, finances, marriage, etc.), so that these changes can be reflected in your financial plan.

know your own financial objectives and risk tolerance.

As a client, you should know your own financial objectives and risk tolerance when you make investments. Your risk tolerance is not the same as your tolerance for taking losses in a market that is going down. Talk this through with your adviser, so you both understand your situation and comfort level.

Do not sign any account opening forms or know-your-client (KYC) forms that you do not understand. Make sure that the forms accurately reflect your preferences.

know what you are investing in.

There are many different investment products in addition to the stocks, bonds and guaranteed investment certificates of previous years. Mutual funds, segregated funds, principal protected notes and exchange-traded funds are popular investments. However, they come in different flavours with wide-ranging levels of risk and can be very complicated. Know what you are getting into beforehand.

review your statements for transaction errors and the performance of your investments.

You should review all transaction records to ensure that the buy or sell order was put through accurately and that you got what you wanted. Review your statements periodically so that you are aware of the performance of your investments. If you have concerns, raise them with your financial adviser. Don't be afraid to discuss whether a change is needed to reflect your needs and comfort level.

know you have the right to complain.

Give your investment adviser and his or her firm a chance to make it right when you have a complaint. If he or she cannot or will not make it right, then escalate your complaint. Most of Canada's regulated investment firms are required by their regulators to have an internal complaint handling process. They are also required to be a part of an external independent complaint handling process, the Ombudsman for Banking Services and Investments (OBSI), which can review your complaint for free if you are unable to resolve it with your investment firm.

CHAPTER 26

How to Fight for Your Rights as an Investor

By Anthony Pichelli

Anthony Pichelli is a certified management account and former investment adviser. He is president of Investment Loss Recovery Group in Toronto.

always be professional.

When people lose money and find that the investment firms are not listening to them, they tend to get very emotional. It will not help your case if you begin to insult the individuals handling your claim at these investment firms. I have seen it happen and the firms will play hardball with you if you do.

document everything.

Keep a record of all e-mails between you and your adviser and make notes of any phone conversations you had with him or her. Make sure you date it and write down the time you spoke, what you discussed and the outcome. Doing so will add more credibility to your claim.

be factual with your claim.

Most investors lose money because an investment is unsuitable for them. This means the investment is not aligned with their risk profile or investment objectives. You must be able to show clearly that the investment was unsuitable for you and that the investment adviser contributed to the loss.

be realistic with your demands for compensation.

It is unlikely that you will recover *all* your losses. In my experience, investors typically recover 30 to 75 per cent of the amount lost, depending on how solid the case is. If you take a hard stance and insist on recovering the entire amount lost, you will not win. Understand how to calculate your losses.

Your loss can be attributed to a particular investment or a basket of investments. Under the most basic loss calculation, you take the amount you paid for a particular investment and subtract the current market value or the amount you sold it for. You can also look at the opportunity cost, which refers to the return you would have received if you had more suitable investments. This is more difficult to calculate and requires making some assumptions.

get professional advice.

When you are trying to recover an investment loss, there are so many moving parts that it becomes difficult to battle these investment firms. I recommend seeking advice from professionals who are skilled at recovering investment losses, such as lawyers and accountants, in order to maximize the amount paid.

CHAPTER 27

How to Recover Losses on Unsuitable Investments

By Ken Kivenko, Small Investor Protection Association (SIPA)

Ken Kivenko is a SIPA volunteer. He's also president and CEO of Kenmar, which provides consulting services to small- and medium-sized enterprises and acts as an investor advocate assisting investors who have been wronged.

WHEN FINANCIALLY UNSOPHISTICATED investors meet commission-driven or quota-driven dealers, a toxic mixture is created. So, it's natural that problems will develop due to greed, misrepresentation, incompetence or even fraud.

An effective investor complaint approach is necessary if you want to recover undue losses. Here are my best tips:

- Expect the investment firm to adopt a 3D approach: Deny, Delay and Dispute.

- Assume your interactions will be adversarial. Check your rights. Make sure you have the facts straight. And have your records available before you complain.

- Get help in framing your complaint. Talk to those who have gone through the process. Contact investor advocates. Speak to a paralegal or lawyer. Do an Internet search. You want to show that your complaint is informed, credible and on solid ground.

- Be respectful, but firm, on what you expect. Financial institutions rarely concede easily or promptly, so prepare for stonewalling. They may try to intimidate you by writing a formal looking letter, saying that you were a knowledgeable investor and were aware of the risks involved and, therefore, do not have a valid claim.

- Don't be put off by these manoeuvres, as they are often ploys to get you to go away. Pursuing a complaint requires determination and knowledge of your rights.

- Complaining to a regulator can help move your complaint along, but won't by itself get your money back. For most retail accounts, the applicable regulators are the Investment Industry Regulatory Organization of Canada (www.iiroc.ca) and the Mutual Fund Dealers Association (www.mfda.ca).

- If the investment firm can't satisfy you, you can use IIROC's binding arbitration process (which can award up to $500,000 in compensation to the investor) or the Ombudsman for Banking Services and Investments (www.obsi.ca) if the dealer is a participating firm.

Often, the negotiation process gets stalled, as investment firms hope to wear you down. Here are a few tactics you can use to get things moving again. All can be time-consuming and will likely add to your aggravation level:

- Contact independent board members of the firm.

- Contact provincial securities regulators.

- Contact professional accreditation organizations.

- Go to the media in an attempt to shame the firm into action.

- Post details of your alleged maltreatment online, but don't make libelous, profane or unsubstantiated comments.

- Tie in with consumer groups and garner their support.

- Picket the firm's offices, as did the victims in the Earl Jones case. This Montreal-based financial adviser was sent to jail after being convicted of operating a Ponzi scheme, which used money from newer investors to pay older investors.

- File civil and/or criminal charges via a lawyer.

- Use social media, such as Facebook, to bring victims together. Brian Hunter, a Calgary oil and gas engineer, used Facebook to create a coalition of 1,800 investors in asset-backed commercial paper (ABCP), whose funds were frozen after the U.S. subprime mortgage market collapsed in 2008. He helped win a settlement that favoured their interests.

- Go to a public company's annual general meeting of shareholders. Buy a single share, if necessary, and disrupt the meeting to talk about your issue.

CHAPTER 28

How to Fight Back Against the Canada Revenue Agency

INCOME TAX IS one of your greatest expenses over your lifetime. But the tax system is complex and not well understood by average taxpayers. You may not know enough to enjoy all the tax savings available to you. Even worse, you may not know enough to avoid making mistakes that can cost you money.

If you make a mistake, you will find that the Canada Revenue Agency is a formidable foe. You cannot avoid its demands. You have little ability to challenge or appeal its rulings. You can become impoverished trying to come up with the money demanded in taxes, interest and penalties. You may even have to declare bankruptcy.

Margaret Williams has a story that sticks in my mind. She cashed in her Registered Retirement Savings Plans (RRSPs) when living outside Canada and did not pay enough tax. She did not realize that she owed more than the withholding tax deducted at source by her financial institution.

The Canada Revenue Agency took nine years to catch up with her and demand the taxes owing. By then, she owed almost $18,000, and about half of that was interest. She tried to pay by instalments, but the CRA wanted its money right away.

"The tax collector used the information on the cheque I provided to contact my bank, freeze all my accounts and confiscate every cent I had in the accounts," she said, adding that she had to borrow from friends to make ends meet.

Following her husband's work, she moved once a year for 10 years and eventually became a non-resident of Canada. She did not tell the CRA about her new addresses each time that she moved.

After she was away for a few years, the international tax office of Canada reassessed her and decided that not enough tax had been paid. But it sent a letter to her in England, where she was no longer living.

In 2003, she divorced her husband and moved back to Canada. She paid her income tax each year, so the CRA had her current address. But the Canadian and international tax offices were not talking to each other, so her new address was not passed from one to the other.

It took until November 2009 for her to be notified of the taxes owing. She had a verbal agreement to pay a lump sum by January 30 and the rest in three monthly payments. But when her first cheque was late because of a mail delay, the CRA emptied her bank accounts.

Williams received an apology when I asked the CRA to review her case. She was awarded the interest from 2003 to 2010, since the CRA said it was at fault for the delay in notifying her of the reassessment.

In another story, Anna Ejbich (then 88 years old) filed her tax return and sent a cheque for $832 in tax owing in 2009. The CRA said she had made a mistake and sent her a refund of $3,032.

"Eight months later, they wrote to me and said they'd made a mistake. They demanded I pay them $3,438, which included $113 in interest on the money sent in error," she said.

Ejbich sent letters to the Prime Minister, Leader of the Official Opposition, Minister of National Revenue, Liberal and NDP revenue critics, CRA Commissioner and her Member of Parliament. She said she was a law-abiding taxpayer who submitted her return well before the tax deadline and attached a cheque, which the government rejected.

"Therefore, I am sure you will agree it is unreasonable to penalize me by charging interest on a mistake that was not mine," she told the revenue minister.

The $113 in interest was waived by ministerial discretion, her son said a few weeks later. He was happy that the media took up her case and helped to get it resolved.

Here is some advice to help you avoid getting on the wrong side of the Canada Revenue Agency:

- Check out the online resources provided at the CRA's website, www.cra. gc.ca. While some publications are fairly technical, others are written in the type of everyday language that anyone with a high school education can understand.

- Always update your address with the CRA when you leave Canada for another country, so that any letters will get to you promptly.

- If you are living outside Canada, check out two publications that lay out your tax obligations: T4056, *Emigrants and Income Tax*, and T4058, *Non-Residents and Income Tax*, at the CRA's website, www.cra.gc.ca. Do a search for the document numbers.

- If you cannot reach an agreement with the CRA, you have the right to ask for a formal review of your case. The review process differs, according to what is in dispute. Go to the CRA website and search for a page called "Complaints and Disputes."

- Check out publication RC17: *Taxpayer Bill of Rights Guide: Understanding Your Rights as a Taxpayer.* This is also at the CRA website, www.cra.gc.ca.

- If you have a service-related complaint that has not been resolved by the CRA, submit a complaint to the Taxpayers' Ombudsman at www.oto-boc.gc.ca. You can print the complaint form, along with supporting documents, and send it by fax or mail to the Office of the Taxpayers' Ombudsman.

CHAPTER 29

How to Avoid Getting Penalized on Your Tax-Free Savings Account

MANY CANADIANS OPENED a tax-free savings account (TFSA) after the product was launched in January 2009. Financial institutions promoted the TFSA as a great way to keep more money in your pocket. Since interest rates were at record lows, everyone wanted to stop paying tax on their meagre interest income.

The Canada Revenue Agency gave information about the TFSA rules, especially the fact that the maximum contribution was $5,000 a year. Banks told their customers not to exceed the limit and most people seemed to get the message.

But another key fact, which should have been emphasized, got lost in the shuffle. As a financial journalist, I mentioned it in my columns. However, I did not appreciate its significance until June 2010, when the CRA sent out tax assessments to those who had put too much money into their TFSA.

Here was the thing that many people overlooked. Once you reached the annual maximum, you could not withdraw money and replace it in the same calendar year. Doing so would count as an over-contribution and result in paying 1 per cent to the CRA.

A penalty of 1 per cent for an over-contribution does not sound bad. But you can understand its impact only if you see how it is calculated. Here is an example that reflects the experience of many of my readers and my adult son (who also got caught).

In January, you put $5,000 into your TFSA. You have already paid tax on this money, so you do not get a tax deduction for a TFSA contribution (as with an RRSP).

In February, you withdraw $5,000 from your TFSA. You need the money to pay an unexpected bill or contribute to an RRSP.

In April, you come into a windfall and you decide to put $5,000 back into your TFSA. You do not think you are going over the limit.

You get an assessment notice from the CRA in the following year with an eye-popping bottom line. You find out that you owe far more in tax than you have earned in interest or investment income that year.

In April, you were $5,000 over the limit and you owe $50 (1 per cent of your over-contribution). In May, you were $5,000 over the limit and you owe another $50.

In total, you owe $450 for nine months of over-contributions in that calendar year. The CRA will tell you to check your records and speak to your financial institution to make sure that the numbers are correct.

More than 70,000 TFSA contributors received such letters in 2010, more than 100,000 received such letters in 2011 and 76,000 received such letters in 2012. The problem is becoming chronic. The government promised to be lenient with those who made an honest mistake because they did not know the rules.

The Taxpayers' Ombudsman, J. Paul Dubé, weighed in on the TFSA over-contribution mess in a 2011 report, *Knowing the Rules*. He called for more communication between financial institutions and the CRA. And he said that the CRA should not only publish information, but also ensure that Canadians could find the information.

Here are ways to avoid a big penalty for over-contributing to a TFSA and to fight back if you get an assessment notice:

- Go to the Canada Revenue Agency's website to find information about the tax-free savings account, www.cra-arc.gc.ca/tfsa.

- Check out a section called, "Contributions, withdrawals and transfers," which has two examples on replacing withdrawals.

- Know the rules on transfers from one financial institution to another. There are no tax consequences if an institution does a direct transfer on your behalf. But if you withdraw the funds yourself and contribute them to another TFSA, this would not be considered a direct transfer and could have tax consequences.

- Keep excellent records. You have to keep track of the money going into and coming out of your TFSAs every month.

- Do not expect financial institutions to warn you that you could be contributing too much. They argue that they cannot keep track of TFSA accounts that may be held at other financial institutions.

- Do not rely on the CRA to warn you about over-contributions. Its letters go out six to eight months after the end of a calendar year. That is too late to help change your behaviour and lower the tax.

- If told that you owe tax on an excess TFSA amount, write a letter to the CRA. Explain why you broke the rules. To bolster your case, ask your financial adviser to write a letter on your behalf.

- Check out a section called "TFSA return and payment of taxes" at the CRA website. It explains the three options available to you when you are told about an over-contribution.

- Finally, if you disagree with a CRA assessment, you can make a formal objection within 90 days of receiving the notice.

- Read the online publication P148: *Resolving Your Dispute: Objection and Appeal Rights under the Income Tax Act*. It's posted at the CRA website.

CHAPTER 30

How to Fight Back by Using the Taxpayer Bill of Rights

By J. Paul Dubé

J. Paul Dubé, Canada's first Taxpayers' Ombudsman, was appointed in February 2008. The position was created to support the priorities of stronger democratic institutions, increased transparency and accountability and fair treatment to all Canadians.

The Ombudsman is an independent and impartial officer who reviews complaints from people who believe they have been treated unfairly or unprofessionally by the Canada Revenue Agency (CRA).

know your rights.

The Taxpayer Bill of Rights outlines what you can expect in your dealings with the CRA. Knowing the service and treatment you are entitled to before you deal with the CRA can help you make the most out of your interactions.

be prepared.

Be clear about why you are contacting the CRA. Have pertinent information and documentation on hand when you contact the CRA. This can include your income tax return; Social Insurance Number (SIN);

Business Number; GST/HST registration number; and correspondence from the CRA relevant to your inquiry or complaint.

be calm and respectful.

Tax issues can be complex and dealing with them can be stressful.

If you feel you have been treated unfairly and you are contacting the CRA to make a complaint, your emotions may be running high. Remember that the agents you are speaking with are likely not responsible for, or even aware of, the situation you are seeking help with. They are there to assist you. If you are disrespectful or take out your frustration on them, you make it difficult for them to understand your situation and provide the assistance you require. Be honest, and do not exaggerate or withhold information.

ask phone agents for their identification.

When you contact the CRA's call centres or general inquiries line, you are entitled to know the identity of the agent who is handling your call. Ask the person for his or her first name, agent identification number and regional suffix.

This information will reinforce the agent's accountability and may be helpful if, at a later date, you have to prove that you spoke with an individual at the CRA or confirm that you received advice.

keep a record of your communications.

Make detailed notes of all your communications, written or verbal, with the CRA, including dates. If you deal with the CRA by phone, make a written summary of the conversations. Note the name of the phone agent, any forms you need to submit, any actions to be done by the CRA and any dates or deadlines.

Keep all correspondence that you send to, and receive from, the CRA. A record of your dealings with the CRA may come in handy at a later date if a dispute arises regarding what was discussed.

attempt to resolve the issue.

Before contacting the OTO to file a service complaint about the CRA, you should try to resolve the issue with the CRA employee you have been dealing with or call the number you've been given.

If you are not satisfied, speak with the employee's supervisor. If you are still not satisfied with the way your issue is being handled, complete Form RC193, "Service-Related Complaint" to file a formal complaint. For more information, visit the subsection of the CRA website, www.cra.gc.ca, titled "CRA—Service Complaints."

If you remain unsatisfied with the way in which the CRA has handled your service-related complaint, you are encouraged to contact the Office of the Taxpayer's Ombudsman (OTO).

contact the OTO for assistance.

The OTO provides a final, impartial review of a service-related complaint after the CRA's internal complaint resolution mechanisms have been exhausted. If you are not sure if your complaint falls within the ombudsman's mandate, or if you have any questions, you can call the OTO and an Officer will be pleased to assist you.

submit a complaint.

Complete all applicable areas of the complaint form at our website, www.oto-boc.gc.ca, before submitting it. Most important: Sign and date Section 3 of the form, "Consent to Disclose Information" to authorize the exchange of information between the OTO and the CRA for the purpose of reviewing your complaint.

If you are designating a representative to act on your behalf, provide the identifying information for your representative. Both you and your representative must sign and date Section 4 of the complaint form, "Third-Party Authorization."

If you have any difficulty completing the form, please contact us.

consult the *Digest* of Taxpayer Service Rights.

The *Digest* is a valuable reference tool for taxpayers wishing to better understand their rights to service and fairness when dealing with the CRA.

You can find the *Digest* at the home page of the Taxpayers' Ombudsman website, www.oto-boc.gc.ca.

The *Digest* demonstrates how the Taxpayers' Ombudsman works to ensure that taxpayers receive the professional service and fair treatment they are entitled to from the CRA. Central to the ombudsman's mandate is to promote and uphold the eight service rights within the Taxpayer Bill of Rights.

PART 3

taming your telecom costs

YOU WANT TO SAVE for the future, but you think that you have noth‐
ing left to cut in your household budget. Think again. Add up what you
spend on telecommunications—your land line and wireless phones, long-
distance calls, cable or satellite TV, Internet service at home and mobile
Internet—and you may see that it takes up a larger share of your monthly
expenses than you realized.

Overspending is common, since there's a continuing flow of devices
that make you want to upgrade. Telecom firms tempt you with new tech‐
nology and then rope you into long-term contracts that subsidize the cost
of your purchase.

Wireless is the fastest-growing telecom category. Canada has three large
wireless companies (Rogers, Bell and Telus) with the financial strength to
build networks across the country. They compete for market share, but they
don't compete on price, except with their bargain brands. Rogers has Fido
and ChatR, Bell has Solo and Virgin, and Telus has Koodo.

The wireless phone companies offer huge subsidies for those who agree
to a three-year contract. There's a good reason why they reserve their best
discounts for longer terms. The longer the contract is to begin with, the
larger the penalty for breaking it will be. They can make extra money by
charging you for an early exit or an upgrade.

The SeaBoard Group published a 2010 report, *Death Grip*, which said that Canada's wireless phone companies impose overly long contracts. In the United States, a typical contract is 24 months; in Britain, it's 18 months. As a result, the penalties we pay are "downright Draconian."

The federal government has refused to rein in the overly long contracts with oversized penalties. Because of its inaction, several provinces have passed their own laws to stop "cell shock." Quebec was the first, followed by Manitoba, Newfoundland, Nova Scotia and Ontario. The provincial laws cap the cancellation fees when you cancel a contract before the end of the term.

Contracts are creeping into other telecom categories as well. These contracts are often verbal only and you get no confirming paperwork. So, you have to ask questions any time your telecom supplier offers you a special promotion or deal.

Suppose you get a call offering discounts on your home phone, TV or Internet service. You agree that you would like to pay less, even if just for one or two years. But if you want to switch to another supplier, you find out that you must pay back all the discounts you have received. Even if you did not sign a contract, you are locked in all the same.

You have to remember that big telecom firms, as do big banks, want to get a greater share of your wallet. Their primary tactic is to offer discounted rate plans if you move services from other suppliers. The more services you have with the same company, the more you save in bundle discounts. But bundle discounts can also keep you captive.

Surviving and thriving as a customer means never letting up the search for the best rates. Instead of settling for the first deal that your supplier offers you, always ask if you can do better. There may be better deals available, but you have to use your bargaining power to get one.

CHAPTER 31

How to Negotiate for Better Rates
with a Telecom Supplier

IF YOU WANT TO TRIM your telecom costs, you have to walk a fine line between accepting long-term contracts and holding on to your freedom to leave. The smartest strategy is to call your supplier every six months—instead of waiting for a call—and doing your own negotiations.

There's a delicate dance you must learn to do, similar to haggling with a car dealer.

First, suggest that you plan to leave if you cannot get better rates. Don't be aggressive. Be polite and seek information. The company expects such calls and save its best deals for clients who appear to be headed out the door.

Second, ask for the loyalty or retention department. You have to escalate to a higher level than the call centre, which lacks the power to give you the lowest prices. You should get ready for this conversation by doing research on the Internet and finding out what rival companies charge for the same package of services.

Third, try to determine your supplier's bottom line, the best deal that it is prepared to offer. You can learn what other people are getting when they drive a hard bargain by going to popular telecom websites, such as Howard Forums, www.howardforums.com, and DSL Reports, www.dslreports.com. Search for "retention" or "loyalty" to see the rates that companies will give to clients they want to keep.

Fourth, avoid getting into a long-term contract that prevents you from leaving if you find a better deal elsewhere. Insist that you will accept only a one-year deal, knowing that you can always call to renew it a year later.

I know that you may find it stressful and time-consuming to call your telecom suppliers every few months to ask for better rates. But unless you play the negotiating game, you will inevitably pay too much for your services.

Here is an example of overpayment. Many people sent me protests when told by Bell that they would pay $2 a month to get statements in the mail. They had to register for electronic billing to avoid the charge. Bell sent the notices in March 2012 to customers with Internet service, though they may have had phone or TV service as well.

I forwarded the e-mails to Bell's executive office, which called customers and offered cost savings to offset the paper bill charge. Some people were surprised to get a large discount on their older rate plans that had not been updated. So, it always pays to ask for a reduction.

Here are a few questions to ask:

- What exactly am I paying for? Can I get a breakdown?
- Do you have any new plans that can reduce my costs?
- Do I qualify for any discounts that I am not getting?
- Can I get a better deal if I bring other services to you?
- Do you have any other money-saving tips for me?

Besides lower rates, there is another benefit of doing regular reviews. You can find billing errors or overcharges that have escaped your notice and you can take steps to get them corrected.

The big telecom companies have strict policies about refunds. They say it is the customer's responsibility to check bills, spot mistakes and ask for adjustments. If you wait too long to complain, you will receive a partial refund for three months, six months or a year, at best.

Here's my advice: Sign up for online access to your account so you can monitor your activity in real time. Do not wait for your bills to arrive in the mail. You want to spot any new charges as soon as they are applied and challenge them if you think they are unjustified.

When it comes to taming your telecom costs, you have to be on guard against an industry that always tries to sell more services, lock you into long-term contracts and inflate your bills. From my experience, customers frequently find errors when they check their bills carefully. So, prepare to fight back and negotiate. You can hold your own only by learning to play the game.

CHAPTER 32

How to Cut the Cost of Your Home Phone Service

SOME PEOPLE ARE DITCHING land lines and going exclusively with wireless phone service. But most Canadians still like the superior sound and reliability of home phone service. They are not ready to conduct all their business on a cellphone.

Even if you stick with your land line, you can reduce your spending on local and long-distance calls by playing off one provider against another. You can save big by leaving a major carrier and going to a rival that uses low-cost Voice over Internet Protocol (VoIP) technology.

Here are some tips on getting started:

- Call a few companies offering home phone service. Check their websites to see what they offer. What is the basic monthly rate? Are some long-distance calls included?

- Many home phone providers use a technology called VoIP that can result in dropped calls, delays and muddiness. Look online to find customer reviews for each company and find out if quality is an issue.

- Once you find a deal that meets your needs and saves you money, call your existing provider and suggest that you will leave unless you get an offer that matches or exceeds what you have found.

- If you feel that your existing provider does not take you seriously, ask for the loyalty or retention department. These people can offer special deals that are not accessible to call centre staff.

- Ask what will happen if you drop your home phone service from a bundled plan. Your discounts may dwindle and the cost of your TV, Internet and wireless phone services may jump.

- Do the math before dropping home phone from a bundled plan, since your higher costs may offset your savings.

- If you intend to switch, find out if you are under a contract with your current provider. Unless you ask, you may not be aware that an early cancellation penalty will show up on your final bill.

- Find out if you have to give 30 days' notice. This is standard among large phone companies. Your new provider can arrange the switch to reduce overlapping bills in the first month.

- Ask your new provider what happens if things do not work out. Can you leave without getting into a contract and paying a penalty to return to your old provider? Is there a trial period?

- Ask your new provider if you can keep the same phone number and if you have to pay a cost to port over your number. What if number portability is not available in your area? Are you willing to get a new number in order to switch?

When you leave your legacy home phone provider, you can choose to go to a full-service VoIP provider that installs the equipment for you and sends you bills of about $25 to $40 a month. This usually includes some long-distance calls.

You can also go to an alternative VoIP service, which costs even less. Once you pay an upfront cost for equipment, you can pay almost nothing for local and long-distance calls. You need high-speed Internet at home (not dial-up), but you do not have to leave your computer running to make or receive calls.

Here are some of the major land line alternatives, which you can buy at leading retail chains and at online retailers such as Amazon, www.amazon.ca, and TigerDirect, www.tigerdirect.ca. (Prices are current as of August 2012.)

Ooma: You buy an Ooma Telo adapter for $230. Then you can start making unlimited phone calls across Canada. The calls are free, but you have to pay taxes and fees (the average monthly cost is $4). You can port your existing phone number for $40. This service gets top ratings in surveys by *Consumer Reports* magazine. See www.ca.ooma.com.

MagicJack PLUS: You pay $70 for the adapter and then pay $30 a year with unlimited calls to Canada and the United States. You can use the service without a computer, but you cannot transfer your existing phone number in Canada. See www.themagicjack.ca.

netTALK DUO: You pay $60 for the adapter, which includes service for one year. Afterward, you pay $40 a year for unlimited local and long-distance calls to Canada and the United States. See www.nettalk.ca.

Skype: Known for making voice and video calls over the Internet, Skype can also be used as a home phone with the purchase of a $40 adapter. Skype-to-Skype calls are free. To make regular calls, you can subscribe to Skype Premium and get unlimited calls to a country of your choice for $5 a month with a one-year commitment. See www.skype.com.

An advantage of an Internet-based phone system is that it's portable and can be used wherever a network connection is found. You can take it with you to a second property or even move out of the province, while keeping the same phone number.

Before making the switch, you should be aware that you could lose your phone service in a power failure. Regular phone lines keep working indefinitely when the electricity goes down. VoIP services rely on your Internet connection, which requires power.

Many VoIP providers maintain service during a power outage with an in-home battery backup system, which can keep corded phones going for up to eight hours. It's up to you to ask the right questions: Is there a battery backup system? If so, do I have to pay an extra cost?

Here's another thing to consider. With a regular land line, you have 24/7 access to health care providers, police, fire and ambulance services by calling 911 in an emergency. They can find your location quickly because traditional land lines can only be associated with a single physical address.

If you call 911 with a VoIP phone, you address is not sent automatically to the public safety answering point. The Internet-based provider will call you back to get your address and dispatch the appropriate service.

In a well-known tragedy in 2008, an 18-month-old child died in Calgary after paramedics rushed to the family's former home in Mississauga, Ont.

The operators used the last known address on file after the parents did not complete an emergency call.

Some VoIP providers are incorporating a feature that will automatically ask you if you'd like to change your emergency contact information when you update your billing address. Even if not asked, you should still make sure to update your VoIP provider when you move.

In January 2011, *Consumer Reports* magazine wrote an article about your high-tech phone system possibly going dead in an emergency. Here are some tips:

- Keep extra batteries on hand. They can extend the amount of time that the backup system powers your phones. Buy them from your provider or try to get additional batteries for free.

- Test the backup. Some carriers monitor the backup system and let you know if it is not working. Try plugging in a corded phone, unplugging the modem or network interface power plug and checking for a dial tone. If you cannot find one, check the system or contact your provider.

- Get a cellphone. Choose a service that lets you pick up a signal from your home. Consider keeping extra cellphone batteries. Find a way to recharge the phone when your power goes out, such as a car charger or windup cellphone charger.

- Consider a generator. If you have a backup generator that provides power to some appliances, make sure that one of them is your VoIP phone system.

CHAPTER 33

How to Save Money on Your Internet Service

YOUR INTERNET SERVICE can cost more than you think. Many providers charge a monthly rate, but add steep extra fees if you exceed your monthly limits for the amount of data (or bandwidth) that you use. Known as usage-based billing (UBB), it can result in unpredictable costs if you have a variety of household devices connected to the Internet.

The solution is to keep on top of your Internet usage and to find a provider that offers an unlimited monthly plan without data caps. These plans are still around, thanks to the efforts of a Vancouver-based group called OpenMedia and its Stop the Meter petition campaign.

A controversy erupted in November 2010, when Bell Canada told independent providers using its network to adopt usage-based billing. The CRTC supported Bell's move, but OpenMedia felt that it was unfair to stop small Internet companies from setting their own prices.

About half a million Canadians signed OpenMedia's online petition, calling for the government to stop price gouging. The media played up the issue, forcing Prime Minister Stephen Harper to take notice. He ordered the CRTC to review its decision to force usage-based billing on Bell's wholesale customers.

In November 2011, the CRTC adopted a new regulatory framework that allowed for greater competition and product differentiation among Internet providers. If you need help finding an independent provider, check OpenMedia's website, www.openmedia.ca/switch, where you can find links to companies in the province where you live.

So, how can you keep your household's Internet costs from escalating? Here are some tips:

- Find out how much bandwidth your household uses every month. Then, check your Internet bills or call your provider to find out if you have the right-sized plan for your needs.

- If you are paying for more bandwidth than you use in a month, you can downsize your plan. And if you are using more data than your plan allows, you can go up to the next size.

- Register for online access to your Internet account. Then, check your usage several times a month to make sure you don't go over your limits. Don't wait for the monthly bills to tell the story.

- Ask your provider to notify you about your usage. For example, you can get an alert when you use 75 per cent of your limit and then when you use 100 per cent. That allows you to cut back for the rest of the month or switch to a bigger plan.

- Track your own data usage, instead of relying on your provider to do it. Bell and Rogers have had cases where their usage trackers were inaccurate and gave customers the wrong information. You can find meters that attach to your router and tally your usage.

- If you exceed your data caps on a regular basis, do the math about staying with a big telecom company or moving to an independent provider. Compare the bundle discounts you get with a big company to the savings you get with an unlimited plan.

The CRTC's final decision on usage-based billing changed the framework for how big telecom companies bill the independent providers that purchase wholesale Internet access from them. But OpenMedia is still waging its Stop the Meter campaign.

"Big Telecom's lack of transparency means they're continuing to price gouge Canadians with impunity," says spokeswoman Lindsey Pinto. "Since the decision, these large corporations have been trying to slide in a new backdoor price hike for Canadian Internet users."

The CRTC has responded by looking at more transparency. It will consult Canadians about the need to take confidential information submitted by the big telecom companies to establish wholesale rates and put it on the public record.

"This is huge," said Pinto. "The best guarantee of an open Internet is a policy-making process that is open, citizen-centred and public interest oriented."

Slow Internet service is also an issue. Many customers complain that they are not getting the speeds that their providers promote and that they pay for. *Marketplace* did a test of home Internet service across Canada in November 2007, which confirmed that the advertising can be very misleading.

"Pay attention to two small but important words, 'up to.' Sometimes they can be a shorthand way of saying 'up to a theoretical maximum speed you may not actually experience, because your wires are old, or you have a lot of neighbours sharing the connection, or because we're still upgrading our equipment in your area," the TV show said.

I wrote a column and blog post in October 2011 pinpointing problems experienced by some Rogers customers in southwestern Ontario, who paid extra for higher speeds but did not get them. Here are some tips on how to fight back if you suspect your Internet is too slow:

- Do your own checking at Speedtest (www.speedtest.net). This is a free service which puts sophisticated testing and analysis tools into your hands if you are curious about the performance of your Internet connection.

- Call your Internet provider and report the speeds you are getting. Ask for help in diagnosing your problem. You could have problems with your hardware, such as the modem or router.

- Once hardware problems are ruled out, you can ask your provider if the slow speeds are caused by network congestion. Find out when the congestion might ease up. Are new networks being built in your area?

- If the slow speeds persist, decide what to do. You can leave your provider and move elsewhere. But that is complicated if you have a contract that ties you into a specific term. Are you willing to pay a penalty for an early exit?

- Investigate getting mobile Internet offered by wireless companies as an alternative to the Internet service delivered to your home by phone lines or cable.

- Mobile Internet can be more expensive than traditional Internet, so check the costs for your usage level. Also, many providers of mobile Internet have policies that allow throttling of traffic to ease congestion. This could affect you if you play video games or stream movies on your devices.

CHAPTER 34

How to Cut the Cost of Your Cable TV Service

IF YOU ARE TIRED of paying monthly bills for cable or satellite TV service, you can invest in a high-definition antenna to get what is known as over-the-air (OTA) TV. This works well if you live close to the U.S. border.

Toronto Star reporter Aneurin Bosley's articles about how he switched from cable to OTA were among the most popular ever run at the *Star*'s personal finance website. "The whole set-up cost me about $175, or five months' worth of basic cable. Not a bad price for about 20 channels of HD TV," he said.

Though you do not get as many channels—and you miss some channels exclusive to cable, such as sports or weather—you can still watch TV on your computer or portable devices. You will not lose out on the shows that create water cooler conversations.

How easy is installation? Balancing at the top of a ladder while trying to strap an antenna around your chimney may seem intimidating, but it is manageable for a handy person, Bosley said. Once the antenna is installed, you may need to tweak the direction a little with somebody inside the house watching the signal strength. (Most new HD TVs will have a built-in signal meter. Just check your manual.)

Luckily, there is plenty of how-to help to take you through the process. Just go to YouTube and search for "install HD antenna," where you will find many videos. And if you find it impossible to do the work yourself, you can hire installers who charge from $300 to $700 for everything.

Location is important. You may live in a neighbourhood with tall buildings that block the view to the nearest Canadian and U.S. broadcasting signals. If you are not close to what you want to pick up, you need a big antenna placed as high as possible.

Here are some pros and cons of setting up an OTA system to replace or complement your existing television service:

PROS

- Over-the-air HD broadcasts are free after the initial costs of an antenna (typically $40 to $150). You might also need to pay $40 for a chimney mount and $10 to $30 for an antenna mast.

- The video and audio quality of HD broadcasts are often better than what you would get from cable or satellite.

- Canadians will get U.S. commercials on American channels (great for viewing the Super Bowl ads).

CONS

- Some set-up is required, such as buying and placing an antenna to pick up a signal. A digital TV with integrated ATSC tuner is required to process the signal. ("ATSC" stands for Advanced Television Systems Committee.)

- Reception can be affected by obstacles (tall trees, buildings) and weather (fog, hard rain, snow), but should be better than satellite.

- Station selection is limited. You can probably get the major Canadian and perhaps U.S. stations, but you get few specialty channels, if any. Compare that to the 500-odd stations you'll get from cable or satellite.

- If you do not live close to the U.S. border, you probably will not be able to access the major American stations, such as ABC, NBC, CBS and FOX.

- While there are personal video recorders (PVRs), they are not as easy to use as ones integrated with cable or satellite service.

There's a website, www.otacanada.com, where you can find a map of all the currently operational over-the-air digital TV stations in Canada.

An antenna should always be grounded in case of a lightning strike, Bosley advises. A good professional installer should take care of this, but for home installers a grounding block should always be used. A good hardware store will have one. And it wouldn't hurt to have a surge protector that also has an input and output for coaxial cable.

"I was struck by the amazing picture quality. I didn't expect that it would be better than digital cable," he says. "A friend of mine, who works in television, first noticed this during *Hockey Night in Canada* one weekend. He kept looking at the picture and saying, 'This looks better than mine,' in a somewhat irritated voice, since his television is larger."

The difference is compression. All TV signals are compressed, but cable and satellite signals are more compressed than OTA. To use a gardening analogy, they are trying to move a lot of water through a limited-size hose.

This set-up may not work for a dedicated sports fan, because you will not pick up TSN, Rogers Sportsnet and so on. In a heavy snowfall, you can find that some U.S. stations, notably NBC and CBS, are dicey. But it is perfect for a casual TV watcher.

"I can watch all the network TV shows in beautiful HD while avoiding a monthly bill of $35, which saves about $420 each year. Not bad for a $100 antenna, $75 in supplies and a couple hours with a ladder."

Here are some ways to watch television content and rent or buy movies outside of traditional cable or satellite TV:

- YouTube is the ultimate online television network, fusing user-generated content with professionally produced shows, music videos and trailers. Free to use, it is accessible on computers, smart phones and newer TVs with Internet connectivity.

- Many Canadian television networks stream TV shows, classic programming, news updates and specialty content from their websites (such as CTV.ca, GlobalTV.com and CityTV.com).

- You can use video streaming from Internet sites such as Netflix, Fast Pass TV and SideReel to watch television content and movies.

- Most of the major television providers offer streaming TV services to cellphones and smart phones. The screen is small, but you can still enjoy watching for short periods.

- Apple's iTunes store lets you download high-quality TV shows and movies to watch on your computer, iPod touch, iPhone, iPad or on your television via Apple TV. You have to pay for the content.

- Some video game consoles let you watch on-demand content, such as TV shows and movies. The Zune Marketplace is an online store for Xbox 360. Sony PlayStation 3 owners can get access to the company's Video Delivery Service, which allows paid access to movies and TV shows downloadable via the PlayStation Network.

- You can buy or rent DVD or Blu-ray Disc movies and TV box sets to watch on your HDTV or computer. Many include an extra disc, called digital copy, to transfer to a computer's hard drive or copy to a portable media player, such as an iPod touch or iPhone. You have no commercials and the ability to pause, play and rewind.

Sales of antennas have spiked across the country as Canadians come to realize what you can get over the air, especially if you're in Toronto and have access to more than 30 Canadian and American stations.

If you want to try putting up an HD antenna, either on your own or with the help of a professional installer, check out the OTA forums at the Digital Home website, www.digitalhome.ca.

Within a few years, almost half of Canada's population will be able to receive digital feeds of all North American OTA networks without needing cable and satellite companies as intermediaries.

When the transition to digital TV broadcasting is completed, cable and satellite providers will have to work harder to ensure there is enough compelling and exclusive content to keep subscribers' eyeballs tuned to their services and their sponsors' products. It should be an interesting shakeout.

CHAPTER 35

How to Save Money on Your Telecom Bills and Get Better Service

By Bob Lepp

Bob Lepp is a semi-retired curmudgeon who tries not to give up when faced with companies that mistreat their customers. He has started a small service business for friends and associates, helping to rationalize their telephone, cellphone, TV and Internet bills to ensure they get the best deals possible. Look for Bob's iPad app named Robellus, offering tips and hints to save you money, at the Apple iTunes App Store soon.

if you want to pay less, call and ask to pay less.

As simple as it sounds, if you want to pay less for phone or TV or Internet, call your provider and say, "Before I make a move to a less expensive supplier, I would like to be sure I am getting the best deal possible on my services." I call it Creative Whining 101.

Listen to what they offer. You will be surprised and angered when they pull discounts out of the air, usually for 12 months' duration, just because you ask. Depending on the service you order and the company, you will have to "commit" to a term of one or more years. Ask what the term is and what the cancellation costs are. Then, you can decide if the savings offered are worth the risk that you may have to cancel.

All companies have "retentions" or "loyalty" staff, whose job it is to offer discounts to save your business. Once they see you as a customer who is price-sensitive, they will deal. You need not threaten, yell or beg. Just be pleasant, thoughtful and patient while they come up with an offer.

If you need time to decide, get a confirmation number. Then, call back and discuss it further. If you get no offers, wait an hour to call back and try again. Each person has varying motivation to help you. Get one in a good mood and you will save a lot.

review your needs for the home phone features and options.

There was a time when phone features were inexpensive, a dollar or two per month. Now voice mail is $11 a month or more. You can buy your own answering machine and cancel that feature. Call display is also about $11. You may not need it if you filter all your calls through voice mail. Call back those whom you want to speak with and ignore the rest.

know your actual needs for long-distance minutes and then you will know your cost.

That long-distance plan you bought in 1997 has risen in cost. You likely pay a slightly hidden "network access fee" as well. Many competitors charge 3 cents a minute for U.S. and Canadian calls. Calculate your effective cost per minute, since you likely do not use all the minutes in your plan. If you are paying more than 3 cents a minute, change to a low-cost direct dial supplier.

stay flexible and ready to jump to a less expensive provider.

Do not use an e-mail address that is locked to a provider. Drop that telus.net, sympatico.ca, bell.net or rogers.com e-mail address. It's a one-time hurt to tell all your contacts and change all your log-on names, but it lets you jump ship when the competition offers 50 per cent or more off Internet.

Gmail is great, Hotmail is fine, Yahoo is OK. Pick one that your friends like and get going. You will have easier access to e-mail when travelling without a personal computer and you will never feel locked in to a major supplier for Internet access.

learn how to find out about hidden promotions.

Deal lovers populate various online forums and blogs, where they discuss current offers. It takes some time, but you can save several hundred dollars a year by knowing what discounts are easy to get today. Companies come up with heavy hidden discounts to throw at those threatening to quit.

If you know what the discount percentage is, you can pretend you were offered it and you are now calling back to confirm taking it. The chances that they record an offer every time is slim. So they will assume you got the offer in the past if you know the correct discount.

Act like you know all about the offer and are just accepting it. You will get it, but if not, wait an hour and call back to a different person. Some are easier than others to convince.

RedFlagDeals (for all services) and Howard Forums (for cellular) are two good online forums. You will find lengthy permanent threads opened just to exchange bargains.

learn the art of threatening to cancel (the equivalent of a master's degree in Creative Whining).

A last-ditch tactic is to say you would like to cancel. You do this *only* after you have called several times to ask for a better rate. You have to convince them that you will really cancel. They know the game and may try to bluff you by saying, "OK, let me process that for you." Or they may break and offer the better deal. There is no guarantee.

Be prepared to really cancel *or* be prepared to say you were hasty and need more time to think. Try this only once a year. If you do it more frequently, you run the risk of being annotated as a repeat offender and cut off from deals.

CHAPTER 36

How to Buy a Wireless Phone
without a Contract

CANADA'S TELECOM COMPANIES charge high prices on wireless devices if you go on a month-to-month plan. However, they offer big subsidies on the same devices if you sign a long-term contract. They save their biggest discounts for the three-year term.

A good example is the HTC One X smart phone, which runs on the Rogers LTE network. (LTE stands for long term evolution, a network that was launched in 2011 and is available only in some markets.)

You can buy the HTC phone for $129.99 if you get a three-year contract. If you get a two-year contract, you pay $524.99 to buy the phone—more than four times as much as for a three-year contract. Meanwhile, you pay $574.99 for the HTC phone if you get a one-year contract or if you stay on a month-to-month basis without a rate plan.

To get the best deal on the hardware, you may take a gamble on paying a low amount up front and hanging on to your device for three years. If technology changes before your contract ends, you hope to be able to get out early by paying a small upgrade fee to your supplier.

You can also sell your old device, and the balance of your contract, at websites such as CellSwapper.com, CellOut.ca, CellClients.com and CellPlanDepot.com (a U.S. site with Canadian listings).

Similar to Leasebusters for long-term car leases, these cellphone websites will make sure that your contract is transferred properly. You will not be on the hook if the new customer defaults on payments.

But you can run into unexpected changes during the next three years. Your cost of living may soar because of separation or divorce, job loss or transfer, or an illness or injury that requires time off work. You may damage your device beyond repair. You may lose your phone to theft and never get it back.

So, look at other options than signing a contract and paying cancellation fees. Check out carriers that offer a more limited choice of phones on a month-to-month basis without any contract obligations. Consider buying the device you want from an online or bricks-and-mortar store, rather than having your wireless provider subsidize the cost up front and lock you into a long-term contract.

Cancellation fees are slowly changing. The Big Three providers used to charge $20 a month, multiplied by the months left in your contract, if you left early. Getting out in the first two months would cost you $680 on a three-year contract. This high fee had no relation to the subsidy you received on the phone.

Then in 2010, Quebec passed a law to limit cancellation fees for wireless contracts. Let us say that you bought an iPhone 4 with 16 GB that year. The unsubsidized price was $649, but you paid only $159 with a three-year contract. Your subsidy was $490 ($649 minus $159).

In Quebec, a service provider cannot charge you more than the rebate you were given on the purchase. This means that your cancellation fee is never more than $490, whenever you get out of your contract.

The rebate gets smaller as time goes on. With a three-year contract, you deduct a certain amount from the cancellation fee for each month that you complete ($490 divided by 36 months = $13.61). If you cancel after two months, your cancellation fee is $462.78. After 12 months, your cancellation fee is $326.67.

Some people do not get a rebate on a phone, but still have a long-term contract. Under Quebec law, if they want to leave early, they pay a maximum fee of $50 or 10 per cent of the total amount yet to be paid, whichever is less.

Suppose you have a three-year contract at $30 a month and you want to cancel after a year. The total yet to be paid is 24 months multiplied by $30, which equals $720. Ten per cent of that is $72, which exceeds the $50 maximum fee. So, you pay only $50 to leave two years ahead of schedule.

Once Quebec broke the ice, a few other provinces adopted new rules for cancelling wireless contracts. All are slightly different in their terms, but they try to link the cancellation fees to the original subsidies given to customers at the time of purchase.

The Canadian Wireless Telecommunications Association believes that varying rules in each province can drive up costs for service providers and ultimately for customers. The CRTC has said it will work on measures to protect consumers under a national wireless code.

Even without new laws, the big service providers are already dropping their rigid cancellation fees and linking them to the initial subsidies.

Telus announced changes in June 2011. Rogers followed suit in January 2012 for contracts signed after that date. Both companies ask wireless customers to repay the hardware subsidy if they cancel their service before the contract ends. Telus has an additional administration fee of $50. Rogers has an extra fee of $12.50.

To use the previous example of an iPhone 4 with a three-year contract and a subsidy cost of $490, you would pay $339.17 to cancel your Rogers service after one year (which includes the $12.50 fee). To cancel your Telus contract, you would pay $376.67.

What should you do if you have an older wireless contract with Telus or Rogers with higher cancellation fees (except if you live in Quebec or Manitoba)?

- Pay an administration fee to cancel your Telus or Rogers plan and get a new plan with the same provider. That will eliminate your cancellation fees in the future.

- Add a new feature to your existing Telus or Rogers plan. Then, if you have to sign a contract renewal, you will also have a chance to take advantage of the new policy.

Bell Mobility still charges cancellation fees of $20 a month until the contract ends, to a maximum of $400, and has not yet moved to a system of hardware subsidy recovery. But Bell, similar to other carriers, does recover a data plan subsidy given to customers who order both voice and data plans.

The CRTC is looking at regulating wireless phones. Back in 1994, it decided to take a hands-off approach to the sector, under the belief that there was enough competition. Now it is revisiting that decision. Despite the entry of new carriers, the Big Three still have more than 95 per cent of the Canadian market.

If you are concerned about the stranglehold on wireless competition and you want to encourage more competition, check out a campaign by a Vancouver-based group, OpenMedia, www.openmedia.ca, and sign its online petition, Stop the Squeeze, www.stopthesqueeze.ca.

The petition states: "I call on the government and policymakers to stop big telecom companies from squeezing independent options out of the cell phone market and price gouging. Please stand up for Canadians by enacting policies that promote cell phone affordability and choice."

Here is the bottom line. When a wireless carrier dangles deep discounts on the latest phone in your face, just say no. Remember that life is uncertain. Life can throw curveballs at you. Say yes to staying flexible and don't sign a long-term phone contract.

CHAPTER 37

How a Customer Fought Back Against Cancellation Fees

AL MCGALE WROTE a Facebook post in February 2011. The headline was "How to quit Rogers TV, home phone and Internet . . . NOW." He described how he argued his way out of his Rogers contract without facing fees. The article went viral and was picked up by the mainstream media.

At the time, Rogers was increasing the prices of all his bundled services (TV, home phone and Internet). He had called to ask if he could cancel because his supplier had broken the contract. Here is his advice on how you can do the same thing:

- Do not expect the call centre to help you. Insist on speaking to a manager or supervisor.

- When the company representative says the contract allows for price increases, ask what would happen if the home phone rate went up to $1 million a month. Would that be acceptable?

- Ask the representative to cite the relevant clauses in the contract that deal with changes in terms of service and a customer's right to cancel.

- Find out what the contract clauses mean, since they can be hard to understand. If you think they support your rights, do not take no for an answer.

In McGale's case, he was told by Rogers that a contract clause protected the company. He challenged the meaning, since he believed that the clause protected the customer.

"Rogers may change these terms, and any aspects of the services, upon notice to you. If you do not accept a change to these terms, your sole remedy is to retain the existing terms unchanged for the duration of your commitment period," said clause 15 in the contract then in effect.

"If you do not accept any other change to aspects of the services, your sole remedy is to terminate."

McGale asked if he could keep his existing contract terms unchanged. That option was not available, the manager said. The rate increases were coming.

Was his contract void as a result? The manager put him on hold while seeking help. She came back to say that he could cancel his services without paying any penalties.

Many customers followed the same strategy, but did not achieve the same results. I think that he got his way because he was persistent and refused to back down. Since Rogers wanted to keep him as a customer, it agreed to give him what he wanted.

When McGale's story hit the newspapers, a Rogers spokeswoman said that a rate hike marked a change in an *aspect* of the company's service. But it did not actually change the terms of service and was, therefore, not grounds for terminating a contract.

It seems that there are no clear rules about what is a major change in terms of service that justifies breaking a contract without penalty. It all depends on the facts, which can change from one case to the next.

Here is my advice:

- Go to your provider first. Then, if you get nowhere, file a complaint with the Commissioner for Complaints for Telecommunications Services (CCTS), www.ccts-cprst.ca. You can call toll-free to discuss your complaint at 1-888-221-1687.

- In cases when a large amount of money is at stake, consider hiring a lawyer and going to court to challenge a company's agreement.

- Talk to your elected politicians about passing new rules to rein in the big telecom suppliers. Make a case that changes are needed in areas that are not currently regulated, such as wireless contracts.

- Do not give up on the legislative route. Telecommunications is a federal responsibility, so write to your MP about passing laws to impose tighter regulation of contract abuses.

- Contract law is a provincial responsibility. Many provinces, starting with Quebec in 2009, followed by Manitoba, Newfoundland, Nova Scotia and Ontario, are changing their laws to make it easier for customers to leave wireless phone contracts without excessive penalties. So, write to provincial politicians and ask them to move into the vacuum.

- Always refer to the code of conduct adopted by members of the Canadian Wireless Telecommunication Association, www.cwta.ca. It promises to "protect our customers' rights when we must change contract terms." This means that when phone providers put through a material change that is detrimental to customers, providers will give them the right to terminate a contract without any fees or let them remain on the unchanged contract.

- The CWTA code of conduct applies only to contracts involving wireless devices. You cannot rely on it in a dispute about your TV, Internet or home phone service, even it is with the same company that provides your wireless service.

- If a wireless company will not cancel your contract without fees, contact the Commissioner for Complaints for Telecommunications Services. Howard Maker, commissioner at the CCTS, told me that he relies on the CWTA code of conduct to help resolve disputes about early cancellation of contracts.

CHAPTER 38

How to Save Money with a Prepaid Wireless Plan

YOUR WIRELESS PHONE PLAN can vary in cost from month to month, depending on how many calls you make and how much data you use. There is often a contract commitment and a variety of extra charges that you did not expect when you signed up.

If you use your cellphone once in a while and not all day long, you can save money by switching to a prepaid wireless plan. The Big Three offer prepaid plans, but the best deals come from independent firms, such as SpeakOut Wireless, Petro-Canada Mobility, WIND Mobile and PC Mobile, which have low per-minute rates and no contracts or extra charges.

Frugal Trader, a personal finance blogger, moved to a prepaid plan after getting a smart phone that was paid for by his employer. He wanted to keep his cellphone number, still used by family and friends, but did not want to pay too much for calls. He picked PC Mobile because he could buy a $100 prepaid card for a full year's usage and a new $80 phone.

"What sweetens the deal is that the prepaid wireless plans typically include caller ID and voicemail, two features that we consider essential," he said in a July 2011 blog post at Million Dollar Journey, www.milliondollarjourney.com.

He figured that he would pay $15 a month in the first year (as long as he did not go over 500 minutes) and $8.33 a month in years two and three. The total cost was $380 over three years, compared to $1,080 if he had stayed with Rogers.

"For the occasional cell phone user, prepaid plans are hard to beat," he concluded.

While PC Mobile is part of the Loblaws retail chain, SpeakOut Wireless is sold through 7-Eleven stores and online at www.speakout7eleven.ca. It offers a full year's worth of use on all its prepaid airtime cards before they expire. Local outgoing calls and incoming calls are 25 cents a minute. Text messages are 10 cents each and incoming texts are free. You can add unlimited Internet browsing for $10 a month.

You can find a wealth of questions and answers and users' tips at a website that is not affiliated with the company. The Unofficial SpeakOut Wireless Consumer Page, www.speakoutwireless.ca/speak, is run by a committed customer named Peter Keung, the same person behind another useful site, www.highinterestsavings.ca.

Both Petro-Canada Mobility and SpeakOut Wireless rent bandwidth on the Rogers network. This means you can buy a Petro-Canada or SpeakOut SIM card and use it with an unlocked phone you already own that works on Rogers's GSM network. If you need to buy a phone, SpeakOut and Petro-Canada both offer a choice of Nokia models in the $50 to $100 range.

With Petro-Canada, https://mobility.petro-canada.ca, and unlike SpeakOut, the airtime expiry dates depend on the voucher you buy. Petro-Canada has a $100 voucher that will last a full year.

Expiry dates are important to check. If you do not pay attention to your unused minutes, you may find that your phone company has appropriated your credit balance.

Bell Mobility, along with its Solo Mobile and Virgin Mobile subsidiaries, was served with a $100 million class action lawsuit in May 2012. You can read the statement of claim at www.bellmobilityclassaction.ca.

Celia Sankar of Elliott Lake, Ont., founder of the DiversityCanada Foundation, wanted to fight back after having her credit balance seized on two occasions. Sack Goldblatt Mitchell LLP, a Toronto law firm, is handling the class action lawsuit, which has not yet been certified.

Bell breached its contract by appropriating her credit balance *on* the stated expiry date and not *after* the stated expiry date as its contract specified, she alleges. Bell also violated the terms of Ontario's Consumer Protection Act. A prepaid wireless plan falls under the same definition as a gift card, which is not allowed to have an expiry date.

Sankar said she was pursuing the case on behalf of Ontario consumers who found prepaid wireless the least expensive way to have a phone. Since it does not require a credit card or bank account, it is often the only option for youths, new immigrants, workers on minimum wage, the unemployed, people on disability and seniors on fixed income.

"These are the people who can least afford to have their funds forfeited or to have their mobile services cut off," she pointed out.

Here are some tips on saving money with a prepaid wireless plan:

- Do your comparison shopping. Check out websites, such as www.comparecellular.com and www.cellphones.ca, where you can analyze costs and features of all the prepaid plans in your area side by side.

- Keep track of your monthly usage. Do not wait for bills to arrive in the mail. Go online and see how many minutes you are using and whether or not you need to top up your plan.

- Always ask if you can roll over your unused minutes to the following month without the risk of losing them.

- If you are a light user, you do not want to waste money paying for airtime that you do not use. So, check out prepaid plans (such as those offered by SpeakOut, Petro-Canada and Wind) that have a 365-day expiry date.

CHAPTER 39

Avoid Data Roaming Charges when You Travel

YOU MAY BE TEMPTED to take your digital device with you when travelling outside Canada. It is useful to check your e-mails and favourite social media websites to keep in touch with what is going on at home. But you can end up with very high wireless phone bills if you do not take some precautions first.

Bill shocks can arise because of a smart phone's data roaming features. Your Internet applications will update themselves automatically when you turn on the phone, even if you do it just once or twice during a trip, pushing up your charges.

For example, a couple named Elizabet and Yails took their smart phones with them during a one-week trip to Arizona in 2011. They later found they had incurred whopping data roaming charges of $1,421 after using 204 megabytes (MB) of data. They asked me for help with Rogers, their wireless provider.

Rogers agreed to reduce their charges by assuming that each spouse had purchased a prepaid U.S. data travel package. The cost was $60 for 75 MB of usage. They were charged only for their over-the-limit usage at 80 cents per MB. As a result, the couple paid $184 in data roaming charges while in the United States, a fraction of what they had been charged before.

When travelling with your smart phone, the best advice is to turn off the data roaming setting. You can eliminate surprises by using only free or low-cost Wi-Fi networks in hotels, cafés and public places. (Short for "Wireless Fidelity." Wi-Fi refers to wireless networking technology that allows computers and other devices to communicate over a wireless signal. Wi-Fi is the standard way computers connect to wireless networks. Nearly all computers now have built-in Wi-Fi cards that allows users to search for and connect to wireless routers, according to Tech Terms at www.TechTerms.com.)

"If you're using Wi-Fi on your device but you haven't turned off mobile data you're still connected to the network," Brent Johnston, Telus's vice-president of mobility solutions, said in an interview.

Here are other ways of downsizing your data roaming charges when you travel outside Canada:

- Ask your wireless supplier about buying a prepaid package for the destinations you plan to visit. You may want to get separate plans for data, voice and text messages.

- Get a prepaid package with a generous limit. The overage fees can be very high if you exceed your limit.

- Look for text messages from your supplier when you cross the Canadian border, advising you to buy a data plan if you have not done so already.

- Look for text messages from your supplier when you are away, indicating that you are getting close to your limit. You can turn off data roaming at that point or opt for a bigger plan.

- Load your own application that will alert you if your data usage goes above a pre-set limit. For example, the Threshold app sells for $3.99 at the iTunes store, and at www.thresholdapp.com.

- Unlock your phone if you plan to leave Canada for a long time. This allows you to remove the data chip (known as the SIM card) and buy a low-cost SIM card abroad, so you can take advantage of local rates.

- Check with your supplier about its policy of unlocking phones. Some do it for a small fee ($50 to $75) before a contract ends, while others make you wait until the contract is finished. You can have it done remotely without having to visit a store.

- Think twice about asking a company you do not know to unlock your wireless phone. This can harm your phone and invalidate your warranty.

If you really want to save money and avoid data roaming charges, leave your smart phone at home. You can get caught up on your e-mails and social media websites at a hotel's business centre or at an Internet café. Another solution is to buy an inexpensive phone in the country where you plan to visit and pay in advance for the minutes that you use.

You may not realize how high data roaming fees can be until you get your first bill after taking your wireless device with you on a trip and not taking proper precautions. Do not be a victim of overcharging.

CHAPTER 40

How a Bell Customer Fought a $10,000 Bill for Data Roaming

DR. RUSS MOYER SPENT only 10 days in Israel, but his decision to take along his iPad cost him almost $10,000. He used the tablet computer to take pictures and check Facebook a few times.

"I was told that the iPad was probably updating all the time, since it was not taken off data roaming and was always connected," he said. "What bothered me was that I was never contacted to be told that I was running up a huge mobile bill."

To his surprise, Bell did not send any warnings while he was away, letting him rack up an enormous charge that exceeded the cost of his trip to Israel. When he complained to Bell, he received a $2,000 credit. Hoping to get more, he contacted me.

Moyer already had a data plan for his iPad, covering travel in Canada and the United States. He didn't know that going overseas could be so expensive and that he needed to buy a separate data plan. And while Bell had a warning system for residential customers, it had not yet implemented warnings for corporate accounts.

Moyer, a minister, had a corporate account. And when I argued that he did not know the rules, I helped him increase his refund. Bell applied an international data roaming plan to his account, just as if he had purchased it, and reduced his bill to $1,607. Bell also helped his travel companion, who had incurred $4,000 in data roaming fees on his iPhone, reduce his bill to $707.

You do not have to pay the high data roaming charges that show up on your bill. Here is what to tell your supplier to get a reduction:

- You do not travel very often. As a result, you did not understand how to limit the charges on your smart phone.

- This was your first offense since you do not travel often. You had no idea that the data roaming charges could be so high.

- Now that you know of the potential for high bills, you will definitely take precautions the next time that you travel.

- You are pleading for a concession this time because of ignorance. You understand that your telecom provider will not sympathize with you if this happens again.

One of my readers was shocked to get a $4,500 data roaming bill after coming back from a cruise. Though she had tried to protect herself from extra charges by buying a plan for text messages and another for phone calls, she was not aware of the need to buy a data roaming plan as well. When she asked Bell to lower her bill, she ended up with just over $200 in data roaming charges.

CHAPTER 41

Watch Out for Premium Text Messages on Your Wireless Phone

TEXT MESSAGES ARE a popular way to communicate, but you have to beware of premium text messages or short code messages (SMS), which allow advertisers to communicate with you through your wireless phone.

Premium text messages incur extra charges, ranging from $1 to $10 apiece, in addition to standard fees charged for regular text messages. Some people who get these premium text messages have never sent a text message before. They do not even know how to use this feature of their cellphones, but they get caught in the trap when they participate in an online contest or order ring tones online.

When you enter your cellphone number at a website, you may be signing up for a series of premium text messages that will keep coming until you reply with a text message saying "STOP." Some people find quite a few charges on the first monthly phone bill they get after signing up.

Canada has a double opt-in system, which means that you have to give your consent twice in order for your text message subscription to go through. The rules are enforced by an industry group, the Canadian Wireless Telecommunications Association, which is responsible for screening companies that want to offer premium text messages. Check its website, www.cwta.ca.

Because of an increasing volume of consumer complaints, the CWTA and its members have introduced new safeguards, such as:

- A $40 monthly cap on a subscription to premium text messages.

- Disclosure of a third-party company's address and phone number on your cellphone bills. This gives you other ways to stop a subscription if a text message does not work.

- A requirement that you have to send a text message saying "YES" to activate a subscription. You also have to click a box saying that you understand the terms of the premium text message deal.

- A time limit of six months on a subscription to a premium text message service.

Some wireless phone companies allow customers to block all premium text messages. This means that you will not get into trouble if you enter your cellphone number into an online form by mistake. Some will block even regular text messages, which can be helpful if you never use them.

These industry safeguards have not been not enough to avoid legal action. In September 2012, the federal Competition Bureau said that it would seek $31 million in customer refunds and penalties from three big wireless carriers (Bell, Rogers and Telus) and the CWTA. It alleged that the carriers were enabling providers of premium texting services to trick people into paying fees that they were not expecting.

Still, it is easy to fall victim to subscription scams if you are not careful. Here are some ways to protect yourself from scams while online:

- Guard your cellphone number as carefully as you guard your credit card number. Don't send your cellphone number to any company that offers an online contest or group purchase. Stay away from promotions that require your cellphone number as a way to participate.

- Scrutinize each monthly cellphone bill. Ask your family members, especially teenage children, to do the same thing. Look for a premium text message, short code message (SMS) and calls from numbers with only four, five or six digits.

- If you find unwanted text messages, do not just delete them. You have to ask the sender to cease and desist. Reply to the message with the words "STOP," "UNSUBSCRIBE" or "END." Save the company's opt-out instructions, which it has to provide, and use them when you want to end your subscription.

- Call your cellphone provider to complain and ask for a refund. You have a shot at getting the premium text message charges reduced or eliminated if you have never complained before. Insist that the third-party sender did not give you a chance to opt out twice, as required by the CWTA's rules.

- File a complaint with the Commissioner for Complaints for Telecommunications Services (www.ccts-cprst.ca).

- Find out if your premium text message service has been approved by the Canadian Wireless Telecommunications Association (www.cwta.ca).

- Ask the CWTA to verify that you subscribed to the service. It can do so by getting access to carriers' records in a dispute about using the opt-in process.

- Read the fine print before you sign up for or click "accept" to any online offer. I know this can be time-consuming and tedious. But many tricks can lie in wait for you unless you make an effort to read a company's disclosure statement.

CHAPTER 42

How to Get the Best Value for Your Telecom Dollars

By Kim Walker

Kim Walker is the ombudsman for Rogers Communications. In her role, she is focused on driving improvements to the Rogers customer experience by providing an impartial, professional review of unresolved customer complaints and investigating both sides of an issue to help ensure a fair and reasonable resolution.

do some research before you buy.

Read online reviews, ask other consumers, check websites for features that are important to you. Try Cellphones.ca for Canadian wireless company information.

get "special" deals in writing.

If you are being sold a non-advertised offer, request a written confirmation before accepting.

look for insurance or equipment protection plans.

In the unfortunate event that you need an urgent replacement, know your options ahead of time.

read the company websites.

You can find loads of helpful tips, community forums, travel information and the latest red-hot deal.

understand how data is consumed on your phone/tablet.

Does streaming a TV show at home use more or less data than using your GPS in the car? Wireless providers offer helpful guidelines right on their websites.

take advantage of usage trackers.

Remember that voice, SMS and data are all different. Download tracker apps to your phone and use them to monitor your usage to make sure you are always on the best plan for your needs.

use plan estimator tools.

We're not all experts at predicting our monthly phone use. But using plan estimator tools can help you decide if there is something better out there for you. Check out Cellplanexpert.ca.

go to online tech forums.

When you need help learning how to use your new tablet or setting a feature on your BlackBerry, tech forums are the fastest and easiest way to learn tips and tricks. My personal favourite is Geek.com.

protect your privacy.

Use a PIN to get additional security on your account. This is optional with most companies, but worth the trouble for privacy of account records.

bundle your services, if possible.

If you deal with a telecom provider that offers multiple services, ask about bundle discounts. Chances are you can save money by sharing plans or household accounts.

CHAPTER 43

How to Cut Your Telecom Costs

By Heather Morgan and Mike Weatherbee

Heather Morgan and Mike Weatherbee are the founders of Cut My Costs Inc., which helps businesses and households trim their telecom and other costs, www.cutmycosts.com. They are paid 50 per cent of the first year of savings that they find for their clients.

research, research, research.

Many people pay too much for telecom services because there are so many options and they don't have the time to figure out whether or not they are getting the best deal—*even after they have spoken directly to their service providers.*

find a solid base.

You cannot be expected to have full knowledge of all the best rates available from every service provider. However, if you do the basic upfront research needed to find what is appropriate costing in the industry, this will help you significantly when negotiating rates in all subsequent years.

understand the competitive landscape.

The Big Three Canadian telecom providers and the many new entrants are all hungry to gain and retain your business. Always get a competitive quote before rushing into a decision, and don't be afraid to have these companies fight for your business! Many consumers take the first offer thrown at them and find themselves locked into a contract that is hard to reverse.

know your plan.

When you sign up for a telecom plan, make sure you understand what comes with it. Plans have grown increasingly complex, and with continuing technology advances, there are many options to keep track of. By taking the time to get a good knowledge of your plan, the likelihood of receiving high overage charges or paying for services you don't need will be greatly reduced.

avoid roaming fees.

Telecom companies leave it up to the consumer to take action that minimizes high roaming rates. So, if possible, turn off data roaming on your phone when travelling. Use Wi-Fi to get access to the information you need. And try to outfit your phone with an appropriate roaming package before leaving the country. These actions will help avoid a hefty bill upon return.

For frequent travellers, it is often worth using an unlocked phone device and purchasing local prepaid SIM cards while away. This allows you to use the local network and eliminate roaming fees altogether.

take the time to get things right and don't be afraid to ask for help.

In our experience, consumers often overpay for their telecom services by thousands of dollars each year—especially when several family members are involved. Businesses often overpay on their bills by thousands of dollars each year. Yet simple action, when prioritized, can have a huge, positive impact.

It's important to make telecom costs a priority and get the help you need, whether it is comparing rates with friends, benchmarking against similar firms in your industry or hiring an expert that can do the work for you.

CHAPTER 44

How We Helped a Household Slash Its Telecom Costs

By Heather Morgan and Mike Weatherbee

HERE IS AN EXAMPLE of the big savings we found for a busy professional couple with three children.

Services: Four smart phones, home phone, Internet and cable TV.
Total annual savings: Over $7,000.

The clients felt they were overpaying for telecom services, but they had no idea by how much. Their bills averaged about $1,000 a month. Their usage patterns differed greatly. They didn't have the time to find the best rates and reorganize their plans to accommodate their real needs.

Our first step was to understand what they were paying for and get a detailed analysis of underlying charges and usage patterns.

We were able to identify the following red flags:

- Their bill was a different amount each month.
- They were getting hit with overage charges for exceeding their limits on daytime call minutes, international long-distance calls and texting.
- They were paying for many third-party charges (for services such as ring tones and game subscriptions) at high prices.

We used our databases to gather the best deals offered by each service provider. With this in place, we could find the plans they would need to lower their bills.

The savings came from:

- Taking the time to understand the source of all the charges.
- Highlighting problem areas and eliminating overages.
- Negotiating different terms that better fitted the client's needs.

The negotiations were long, with a lot of going back and forth, and we came close to switching suppliers. But we were able to leverage our clients' history with their provider to get rates that we knew were possible, but were not generally public knowledge.

Since we work with multiple clients and suppliers, we know what's possible. We stick with the negotiations, or the possibility of switching suppliers, until we get the right deal.

As a consumer, you can use a similar process by benchmarking what you have against the rates offered by different suppliers on their websites. You can also seek help from friends and family in comparing the different package deals.

Negotiating with telecom suppliers, despite what they say in their advertisements, is not an easy process. You have to know what you want and what is feasible. Then, you must be persistent and determined to get the deal you are looking for.

The savings: We reduced the family's bill to about $400 a month, down 60 per cent, while increasing their service quality.

How did we do it? We knew that generic plans are not tailored for individual habits. So we found a way to match the family's profiles to the plans. (Different people use their phones in different ways.) It took a lot of negotiation because the telecom suppliers have a cookie-cutter approach to their customers. You have to know what you need and what you can get.

This household already had a contract, but we were able to renegotiate it. We built on the fact that they were good clients and were not getting what they needed.

In general, our clients are happy to be locked into a contract for a slightly longer time if there is an obvious payoff. We recommend extending a current contract by a modest amount if it helps you get much better terms. Of course, this depends on where you sit in a contract and how much time is left to go until the term ends.

CHAPTER 45

How to Make Effective Telecommunications Complaints

By John Lawford

John Lawford is executive director and general counsel with the Public Interest Advocacy Centre (PIAC) in Ottawa. He is active in the areas of telecommunications, financial services and health law from a consumer perspective.

AT PIAC, we've seen a lot of complaints sent to telecommunications companies. Some are good, but most are badly written. Consumers often do themselves a great disservice and let the company off the hook.

Here a few DOs and DON'Ts, based on our experience as advocates for telephone, cellphone and Internet customers in Canada.

do:

Write Your Complaint Out in Detail.

You will need to put factual events in chronological order to send to the telecommunications company. And if you are not satisfied, you can send your complaint to the Commissioner for Complaints for Telecommunications Services (CCTS). Its services are free.

Contact details and procedures are explained online at http://www.ccts-cprst.ca or you can call toll-free at 1-800-221-1687. The Canadian

Radio-television and Telecommunications Commission requires all telecom providers to be CCTS members and live by its decisions. It's as close to a fair judge as you'll get. Trust us, we know.

Retain and Make Copies of All Bills for the Period in Question.

Keep your bills and have them ready. You should attach them to your complaint as evidence, even if your complaint is not about billing.

Keep Detailed Records of All Conversations with Any Employee of a Company with Which You Are Having a Dispute.

Make sure to include time, date and subject details, as well as a summary of what was said. This will be evidence for the company or the CCTS to substantiate your claims. If you don't do this, your conversation never happened. Your word is valueless; your handwriting is gold.

Ask if the Customer Service Representative has the Authority to Take Action to Resolve the Complaint to *Your* Satisfaction.

If you want a refund for poor service, ask the customer service person, "Do you have authority to refund my account (up to $X)?" If not, ask to speak to a manager or someone with that authority.

Find Out About the Internal Complaints Process within the Company.

This may be available from a customer service person or the company website. You need it so that you can escalate or appeal your result if you are not satisfied.

Become Informed About What Competitors Can and Will Offer You.

You may need this information if you plan to threaten to take your business elsewhere. And if you cannot resolve your complaint and do intend to switch, you will be ready.

Threaten to Take Your Business Elsewhere (Even if You Have No Such Intention).

This is the largest weapon in your arsenal, so use it sparingly and as a last resort. If you do, you likely will be transferred to a "retention department" or a "save queue" with representatives that have more authority to resolve your complaint. It costs so much for the company to attract and set up clients that it sees more value in retaining you than finding a new customer.

Be Prepared to Compromise.

There may be middle ground that is less disruptive to you than switching, but still achieves a good result. You may wish to try to compromise only after speaking with the retention department.

Complain to the CCTS in a Timely Way, with All the Details.

If you are still unsatisfied with the company's response, CCTS is there for you to resolve your complaints, so use it. Telecom firms are required to tell you about the CCTS. So, make sure to mention if you were not informed of its existence by the supplier.

don't:

Call a Telephone Company or E-mail an Internet Provider.

Write a good old-fashioned letter on paper and send it to a physical address. (For major telephone companies, there should be an "Executive Customer Service" office address listed in the front of the white pages telephone directory.) If you are worried about receipt, send your letter registered with an acknowledgement of receipt card.

When dealing with smaller telephone companies (and this includes cable companies that might be offering telephone or Internet service, or newer companies offering telephone, cellphone or Internet service), you can call customer service staff or look at the website, but only to get an actual physical mailing address.

If the company tells you it has only a website or phone number for receiving complaints, you should consider switching providers to one that does have an address.

Be Paranoid, Threatening or Abusive.

Dogs, bees and telecommunications companies can smell fear. If your complaint has a whiff of persecution about it, you will be treated as a person better ignored or avoided and not as a valued customer. Avoid phrases such as "you are ignoring me" or "you are threatening my life." (We've actually seen that last one!)

Use All Capital Letters.

If you can't get your message across without shouting, you've already lost.

Writing only in lower case with poor spelling, typos, lack of proper spacing or other mistakes likewise signals you can and should be ignored. Same goes for extraneous exclamation points.

Use Sarcasm.

Surprisingly enough, it backfires. Did you just feel offended by that last sentence? Now you know how the person at the telecom company feels when reading your letter. That person may just drop it into their "special" file, which is round, sits on the floor under their desk and is emptied each night. (Sarcasm again! Fight the urge.)

Send a Carbon Copy of Your Complaint to the Prime Minister, Your MP, MPP, City Councillor, PIAC, the Local Newspaper and Your Mother.

If any of these people can help in the future, you have to tailor your communication to their particular function or expertise. Sending your complaint to them now signals that you don't care about their time, don't care about your own privacy or are naïve about who can help you in life.

Write Anything in a Complaint that Is Unrelated to the Complaint.

Your complaint should be factual. Avoid gratuitous comments on the company's morals, leadership and conduct in the marketplace or general reputation. Avoid threats to individuals or the business in general and accusations of political manipulation by the company.

Give Up.

The telecommunications industry can be exceptionally difficult for consumers to deal with. Taking the time to complain (properly) is your best option for getting these companies to collectively pull up their socks.

We at PIAC will cheer you on.

CHAPTER 46

How to Fight Back Against Big Telecom

By Lindsey Pinto

Lindsey Pinto is communications manager at OpenMedia.ca, a grassroots organization that safeguards the possibilities of the open and affordable Internet. It is known for coordinating Stop the Meter, the largest online campaign in Canadian history, involving more than half a million people.

WE BELIEVE THAT every Canadian citizen must have access to a high-speed, world-class communications and media infrastructure. Let us all fight together against price gouging by Big Telecom.

(1) Make the switch to an independent ISP (Internet service provider). By moving away from Big Telecom, you fuel competition within the Internet service market and slowly chip away at the unhealthy oligopoly in Canada today. And since some indie ISPs are able to offer unlimited plans, you'll also save quite a bit of money without worrying about data capping!

(2) Consider switching to an independent cellphone provider (such as WIND or Mobilicity) when your mobile contract expires.

(3) File a complaint with the CCTS (Commissioner for Complaints for Telecommunications Services). While we strongly recommend pushing for structural change for our broken Internet service marketplace, this is also an option when you're the victim of unfair practices.

That said, it's unfair that the onus currently falls solely on the consumer to report on telecom companies, because:

- We have no access to data from the ISPs about their traffic management practices.

- It's difficult to know what's needed to file a complaint.

- And it's sometimes hard to get access to the data that would make a complaint credible.

That's why we think the following actions make the most sense:

(4) Become an active member of the pro-Internet community. Fast, affordable Internet is the key to participatory democracy and healthy communities. We all deserve a say in how it is managed. Share your story with others and be a part of a strategy to make key structural changes that will make digital services better for everyone.

(5) Sign and share OpenMedia's petitions against mobile price gouging and metered Internet billing. This will help bring these key issues to the attention of the media and policy-makers.

(6) Keep an eye on the CRTC's proceedings about getting more transparency for Big Telecom and creating national rules to protect wireless customers. They could make a huge difference for you and others who want an open and affordable digital future.

(7) Call or send a message to your MP, detailing your concern with the lack of competition in Canada's telecommunications market. With the market monopolized by Big Telecom, pricing stays high, access stays low and consumers are denied adequate choice.

stretching your travel dollars

TRAVEL MAKES LIFE exciting and memorable. Today, you can explore the world more economically than ever before, as travel providers slash prices to reach bargain-minded shoppers online.

Thanks to the Internet, you can get access to last-minute sell-offs of airline seats, hotel rooms and cruise cabins that would otherwise go unfilled. Some of the best deals involve opaque pricing. This involves getting a deep discount if you can accept some uncertainty, since you have to pay up front without knowing which airline, hotel or car rental firm you will get. You make a booking on a non-refundable basis.

Websites such as Hotwire and Priceline use opaque pricing to dispose of unsold inventory for well-known travel companies. Their names are kept secret in order not to cannibalize their high-price brands.

You can visit far-off places you could never afford in the past by using travel reward points. You collect points on your everyday spending with credit and debit cards and redeem them for flights, cruises, car rentals and hotels. You can also use your points for upgrades to a higher status that was formerly out of reach.

However, there's a big caveat about travel reward points. One day, you may be surprised to find that your account is empty and your dreams of future trips are up in smoke. You can lose your points if you do not manage them carefully. You have to read the rules and not lose points to inactivity or ignorance of the expiry dates.

As consumers, we hope that our trips will go smoothly. But experience shows that there is always a risk of things going wrong. Arrangements can go off-track for a variety of reasons, such as weather, construction, natural disasters or political events. If a trip costs more than planned, who is responsible? How can you settle disputes with a travel provider?

In my experience, many large travel companies like to stonewall when they get a customer complaint. They often insist that you communicate in writing only and wait for a response, which can take weeks to arrive. If they do agree to compensate you, they usually do not give a refund or rebate. Their favourite tactic is to offer a discount on future travel.

This stinginess by airlines, tour companies and hotel chains forces you to seek legal help if you want your money back. Going to court is often the only way to make travel companies give your money back for providing substandard service. They know there is a good chance that you will never use the discount vouchers you are offered. The last thing you want to do is patronize the same company again.

Debbie Boukydis tried to get through to Celebrity Cruises after her luggage went astray for a week, leaving her with nothing to wear (and nothing to buy, either). After getting an insulting offer of $300 at first, she fought hard to get the company to offer a free cruise, but plans to give it to her daughter, since she can't stand the thought of taking another Celebrity cruise.

Dave Carroll, a Halifax musician, never did get any compensation from United Airlines for damage to his checked baggage. But he got revenge by recording a series of YouTube videos, *United Breaks Guitars*, which scored millions of views around the world and launched his new career as a customer service advocate.

Besides fighting back against travel providers when things go wrong, you may also have to go to battle with an insurance company when illness derails your plans. You may think that your travel medical policy will pay you back if you cancel a trip before leaving or cut it short while you are away because of a health emergency. But you may find that you have purchased the wrong type of coverage.

Travel medical insurance is a complex product. You have to give information on your health history in a questionnaire that takes time to fill out. You may have to consult with your doctors to make sure that your answers are correct. But you are not always advised to do so by the travel agents selling these policies.

If you make a mistake in any one of your answers, you will not be able to collect on your insurance. All you will get is a refund of the premiums that you paid. You could be left with thousands of dollars in unpaid bills for medical care outside the country, even if the reason for your claim has nothing to do with the erroneous answer.

Travel health insurance providers put the onus on customers to read the policy and disclose all previous health problems. They often use a written disclaimer, saying that one wrong answer invalidates the policy. So, if you forget to mention that your prescription drugs changed or you took a medical test before going on the trip, you are out of luck when filing a claim.

Your only recourse may be hiring a lawyer and going to court to recover those costs. You can go to the health insurance company's ombudsman and, if you are turned down, you can appeal to the OmbudService for Life and Health Insurance, www.olhi.ca. But there's only a slim chance of getting the denial of your claim overturned.

Choose your travel providers carefully. Find firms with a history of excellent service. Read online reviews at websites such as TripAdvisor, looking for comments from customers about how their complaints were treated. If you see signs of excessive stonewalling, back off and look elsewhere.

Chances are that your trip will proceed as planned, with only a few minor glitches. You will not have to send angry letters to companies demanding compensation. You will not have to file claims for lost or damaged luggage or other problems that interfere with your travel.

However, if you do end up with a fight on your hands, you want to know that your travel provider will treat customers with respect, apologize for its mistakes and offer appropriate compensation without a court case. That will ensure a soft landing after a bumpy ride.

CHAPTER 47

How to Fight Back when an Airline Damages Your Luggage

MUSICIAN DAVE CARROLL was flying from Halifax to Omaha, Nebraska, with a connection at O'Hare Airport in Chicago. He had never flown on United Airlines before. Knowing that Air Canada had a policy of checking musical instruments, he did not argue with the United agent who denied his request to take his two guitars with him into the cabin.

The flight to Chicago was uneventful. But upon landing, a passenger looking out the window at the tarmac said words that would make any musician cringe: "Oh my God, they're throwing guitars out there." Mike, a member of Carroll's band, also saw a guitar being thrown to a baggage cart.

A United employee at the terminal told him that he had signed a damage waiver when he checked in, releasing the airline from any responsibility if the instruments were destroyed in transit. Carroll insisted that he had not been asked to sign a waiver. In any case, no waiver he ever signed would make throwing instruments acceptable.

Arriving after midnight in Omaha, he went straight to the hotel to sleep. When his van arrived the next morning, he drove for a few hours with his band to the first tour stop. Only then did he pull out his $3,500 Taylor guitar and see that it was badly damaged.

"I decided my only option was to put the Taylor back in its case and not look at it again until I returned to Omaha, and I was grateful I had my Ovation to complete the tour," Carroll wrote in his 2012 book, *United Breaks Guitars: The Power of One Voice in the Age of Social Media.*

He waited a week to open a claim with a United employee in Omaha. She said she didn't need to see the damage to the guitar and told him to open a claim at the airport where his trip began, in Halifax.

Alas, United had no official presence in Halifax. Air Canada, its partner in the Star Alliance, gave him a United brochure with a toll-free number that connected him to a call centre in India. They suggested that he bring the guitar in to O'Hare for an inspection. No way, he said.

After much confusion, he was told to go back to the Halifax airport to open the claim and have the damage inspected there. Air Canada refused any liability, but promised to pass the paperwork on to United.

Carroll spent seven months chasing United to get help with his claim (from April to November 2008). His final contact was with Ms. Irlweg, a customer service representative in Chicago and a seasoned pro. They danced along for about ten e-mail exchanges before she ended the relationship with "The Final No."

United denied his request for $1,200 in flight vouchers as compensation for the guitar repairs. He should have started the claims process within 24 hours of arriving in Chicago and that was his ultimate undoing. Carroll said that he had reported the damage at his earliest opportunity before being told to bring the guitar back to Canada for inspection.

In his last e-mail to Ms. Irlweg, Carroll said he was not without options. He would write two or three songs about his experience, make videos and post them on YouTube. "United Breaks Guitars," the first performed as a country music "hurtin' song," went up on July 6, 2009.

In the video's defining moment, a broken guitar was placed on the ground and a chalk circle was drawn around it to simulate a dead body. Countless people sent e-mails to Carroll, saying they loved that bit.

He had hoped to get a million views for all three videos combined in the first year. But he reached his goal with a few days. The first video hit the three million mark by the end of the second week, launching a frenzy in the media and forcing United to respond.

Very soon after the video went viral, a customer service manager called to offer the same $1,200 in vouchers that Carroll had asked for, plus an extra $1,200 in cash for his trouble. Carroll refused.

"Although they made no suggestion that accepting the compensation would require that I remove my video from YouTube, or that I would not make the additional two remaining installments, I felt that accepting it would weaken my credibility," he said. "This was now about something bigger."

Carroll's book is a quick read, just under 200 pages, including lyrics to all three United songs. Carroll tells his story with charm and humour, enlivening it with lessons to large organizations about how not to ignore customers. He is now a sought-after customer service speaker and a partner in an online venture that helps consumers and businesses resolve disputes, Gripevine (http://gripevine.com).

Can an average consumer create a YouTube video that will be heard around the world? With the growth of social media, it is harder for unknown individuals to build a mass following. But a few determined and creative fighters will still be able to pull it off.

tips on how to be successful using social media.

By Dave Carroll

Dave Carroll is the musician behind United Breaks Guitars. He is also a singer-songwriter, speaker, author and consumer advocate. His website is www.davecarroll.com.

In order to be successful using social media, you need to create content that (a) looks good, (b) sounds good and (c) makes people want to tell their friends about it.

Though it's easier said than done, you can achieve it if you understand the following tips.

- **Know your audience.** Do you need to reach millions to be successful? Or is your message intended for an audience measured in the dozens? Your approach will need to customized depending on whom you are targeting. Knowing your audience is the key.

- **Cut through the noise.** In a very competitive environment online, with millions of people vying for attention to share their message, you have to be unique to be heard. If you make a video, you must show something others can relate to. Your video has to resonate with a target audience to cut through the noise.

- **Content is still king.** In my research, I discovered many videos with millions of hits. But some had awful production quality and were forgettable after one view. If you ask busy people with short attention spans to consider your message, you have to respect their time by creating good audio and video and getting to the point. I used a song and music video, but whatever way you choose to share your message, good quality content is one of the few things you can control.

- **Use humour wherever possible.** Humour draws people in. Everyone likes to share a joke or funny story with their friends. People will be more likely to share your message if it can make them laugh while educating them. Be funny wherever possible. This will also increase your enjoyment in the creative process. Get rid of your anger and frustration before you shoot the film. Revenge is a negative emotion. Do not be confrontational.

- **Be authentic.** Being yourself when presenting a message is something else you can control. Your message will always be more compelling when you are yourself. When you try to be what you think others expect, instead of "authentically you," it will come across as contrived and your audience will feel as though they are being played. Your story matters. It's simply a matter of presenting it in the right way.

CHAPTER 48

How to Fight Airline Rules That Do Not Make Sense

THERE IS AN INTERESTING footnote to Dave Carroll's story. Remember that United denied his claim because he did not report the damage within 24 hours? A consumer advocate later challenged the airline's right to enforce the deadline and found that it was wrong.

There is no such thing as a 24-hour period for baggage complaints under international conventions, the Canadian Transportation Agency said in May 2012. It was reviewing a complaint by Gabor Lukacs, who found the name tag missing from his suitcase after a United flight from Winnipeg to Savannah, G.A. Although he was given $15 for the missing name tag as a goodwill gesture, Lukacs said the airline could not deny liability for normal wear and tear of baggage.

The CTA is an independent federal administrative body that resolves consumer disputes about airlines, www.cta.gc.ca. It supported Lukacs on the fact that United could not shrug off its responsibility to pay for damage to protruding parts of a suitcase. It also said, in effect, that United was wrong to turn down Carroll's claim.

International passengers can complain to a carrier about damage to checked baggage within seven days at the latest, the CTA said. They cannot be denied compensation because they missed a short window of 24 hours.

As a result, United had to change the information given to passengers about its baggage policy. It now says that damage must be reported in writing to the airline no later than seven days after arrival for international flights.

Lukacs, who lives in Dartmouth, N.S., is a fighter when it comes to lost and damaged baggage. He succeeded in challenging WestJet Airlines' $250 limit on liability in 2010, arguing that Air Canada's limit was a more generous $1,500. A year later, he challenged Air Canada's denial of responsibility for valuables in baggage on certain itineraries. The CTA agreed that it was unreasonable.

Why does he take on airline complaints? Lukacs says he is guided by a firm belief in the rule of law. He travels a lot himself and hopes that his fellow passengers will be treated better than they were before when their luggage goes missing or gets damaged.

He also believes in penalizing airlines for bumping passengers from crowded flights. Thanks to his efforts, the Canadian Transportation Agency has rewritten the rules to strengthen passenger rights.

In a series of decisions relating to Lukacs's complaints, the agency said that you could opt for a full refund or a free trip when your flight was overbooked, delayed or cancelled. The new rules apply to Air Canada, WestJet and Air Transat, but they do not apply to disruptions caused by bad weather or security issues.

"Prior to these decisions, the tariffs of the three air carriers were more restrictive with regards to passenger rights," the agency said in a release in June 2012.

Previously, the airlines had the discretion to decide on a refund or a rebooking when they couldn't fit you onto an overbooked flight. They could choose to reimburse you only for the unused portion of your ticket, rather than the whole thing.

When asked about overbooking, Lukacs gives a blunt answer. "Morally, I view the practice of overbooking flights as a contractual and institution-alized fraud," he tells me.

He supports the regulatory measures taken by the European Union and the United States to reduce bumping by compelling airlines to pay significant monetary compensation to affected passengers.

When airline tickets were easy to change, overbooking made sense to compensate for no-shows. But that is no longer the case.

"Many tickets are non-refundable, so airlines do not suffer a loss if a passenger doesn't show up," he points out. "In fact, an airline makes money because it will be carrying less weight. These days, when an airline oversells a flight, it ends up collecting the fare twice for the same seat."

Here are Lukacs's tips on fighting back against airlines:

- Record your conversations using a digital tape recorder with a lead to the phone. All you need is the consent of one party (yourself). When you call a customer service centre, the call is likely being recorded. You have the right to record your own communications. Such surreptitious recordings are admissible as evidence in civil cases.

- Take detailed notes. These are also usually admissible as evidence in court.

- Ask for written evidence. When an agent refuses to comply with your request, get it in writing. If the agent won't do so, you can create a written record by sending a letter or e-mail to the airline: "We spoke on this date and you advised me that . . . You refused to put this information in writing when I asked." This conveys the message that you are serious.

- Call airline directors and CEOs at home. Corporations usually have to be listed at a provincial registry, free to the public, which has the names and addresses of officers. This lets you find their phone numbers at 411. Call during the day and be polite.

- Learn the laws. Airlines are governed by the Montreal Convention, an international treaty that has the effect of law in Canada and the United States. It sets out their liability in case of damage, destruction, loss or delay of baggage, and injury, death and delay of passengers.

- Do not delay in reporting problems. You have strict timelines to notify an airline. Check the airline's website for information about how long you have to report baggage damage and delays. Try to do it immediately at the airport, followed by a formal letter of complaint.

- Know your rights. Many airline employees confuse their company's policies with the law. If you are familiar with your rights, you can protest. You may end up with the company's legal department, which knows the law.

- Don't ask airline employees about your rights. They often give false or misleading information to passengers. Tell airline employees what your rights are.

CHAPTER 49

How to Fight Back when a Cruise Line Loses Your Luggage

DEBBIE BOUKYDIS WAS looking forward to a relaxing Caribbean cruise aboard the *Celebrity Eclipse* in February 2012. But she came home frustrated and exhausted after the cruise line misplaced her suitcase, leaving her with nothing to wear for a week but the clothes that she wore on the plane.

"I was devastated," she told Celebrity Cruises in a complaint letter. "This bag had all my clothes, formal attire for the evenings, a special Valentine's day outfit, my husband's Valentine's day gift, my bathing suits, cosmetics, shoes—everything, absolutely everything."

Her bag was on the *Celebrity Millennium*, not the Celebrity Eclipse, and she could get it back only when she and her husband returned to Miami in seven days. She asked if Celebrity would fly her home right away, but that would mean forfeiting the cost of the cruise.

The ship manager asked if she had baggage insurance. She had none. Then he offered a $500 credit to be used on the ship to cover the cost of clothing and cosmetics. Unfortunately, there was little in her size and at a reasonable price to buy. She got flip-flop sandals for $110 and some logo T-shirts and pants for $275.

She and her husband ended up missing the formal nights on the ship, which had attracted them to Celebrity in the first place. They had to cancel a prepaid tour of San Juan, Puerto Rico, and argue for a refund, so they could go shopping for appropriate clothing instead. But the search proved to be fruitless.

"I had no luck finding a bathing suit or anything that could be deemed to be suitable for wear in the evenings," she said.

"After shopping carefully for weeks before the trip and planning every day for this beautiful cruise, I was left with two pairs of capri pants—one too big and one too small—and some tops that I never would have purchased in a million years under normal circumstances."

Boukydis had spent her career in communications and customer service at a large natural gas utility in Toronto. She wanted compensation, but could not reach anyone in authority. After finding the name of Celebrity's chief executive, Daniel Hanrahan, she paid $75 to send registered letters to him and two other executives.

"I view the original mistake of loading my luggage on the wrong ship as just that, a mistake. These things happen and we are all human," she wrote to him. "But the way in which your organization responded to my plight was entirely inadequate and disrespectful to me as a customer."

The chief executive did not apologize for the bad treatment. He did not even respond. Instead, Boukydis got a phone call from a Celebrity customer service representative two weeks after her registered letter was signed for in Miami.

"She asked for all my receipts. I said, 'Did you read my letter? I don't have receipts because there was nothing for me to buy.' She wanted to explain to me what happened. I said I didn't care what happened. Then she offered me $300 off on my next cruise. This was an insult, since I had already received offers of $400 to $500 in marketing emails."

The Celebrity rep had 30 minutes to come back with a better offer, Boukydis told her. And if Celebrity did not come back with a better offer in 30 minutes, here is what she would do:

- Write to the eight people on the board of directors, whose names and addresses she found online, telling them what happened and how she was ignored by the management team.

- "If the board of directors of the company I work for had received a letter like that, I'd be fired," she said, adding that the letters were written and ready to go.

- Instruct the consumer columnist at the *Toronto Star* to go ahead with a story. Boukydis had already spoken to me about Celebrity's poor customer service and attracted my interest.

- Work with a communications expert on a YouTube video, showing what she had planned to wear on the cruise and what she actually did wear. "It will make 'United Breaks Guitars' look weak," she said.

When the representative talked about taking time to consult her team, Boukydis replied, "I don't care. I want an answer in 30 minutes or I'll go to the post office to register these letters."

The threats worked. The rep called back by the deadline, saying that Celebrity would give Boukydis a free cruise. "For me only?" she asked. "I want it for my husband and me." The rep agreed on the spot to extend the offer to both spouses.

Boukydis said yes, even though she knew that the Celebrity offer still came up short. She and her husband received a refund of $1,200 each, which covered the cruise but not the airfare. There was no refund for the dining room upgrades that she did not get a chance to use because of wardrobe issues. And the free cruise had a time limit of one year.

"They wanted to get me off their back," she said. "I could have pushed a bit further, but I'd had enough. I don't want to go back on that ship. My daughter and her husband will get the cruise."

In her letter to Celebrity, she said the staff at the Miami airport had tagged the couple's four bags correctly. She had photos of the luggage, showing that the bag that went cruising without her on the Millennium clearly had an Eclipse tag.

Boukydis learned a lesson from the experience, which was reinforced by her friends who had taken cruises. When you land at the airport, the cruise line usually puts your bags on a bus headed to the port and then transfers them to the ship. If you want to ensure that your bags go to the right place, do not let them out of your sight. Insist on taking them onto the bus and the ship yourself.

Susan Pigg, a *Toronto Star* reporter who worked in the travel section, has another tip. When travelling with a partner, divide the clothes between your checked bags. This means that if your bag goes astray, you will not lose everything you had planned to wear. There will be another bag with half of your belongings.

Here are more tips about what to do if your luggage is lost or missing after an airline flight:

- File your claim immediately at the airport, giving information about where you will be staying in the next few days. The airline can track the bags and send them to you en route.

- Before leaving the airport, make sure you know how to check on your bag's status.

- Most missing baggage turns up later. But if your bag is lost and not found, you will have to produce receipts to show the value of the items you lost. Make sure you have backup evidence before taking valuable items with you.

- Airlines often decline liability for some items in checked baggage (such as jewellery, money or antiques). Keep your valuables in a carry-on bag if they are not covered.

- Put a change of clothes into your carry-on bag. Then, you have something to wear if your checked bag is delayed.

- Keep all the documents that you need for travel, such as itinerary and contact information, in your carry-on bag.

- Put together a list of the items in your checked baggage in case you have to make a claim. You can also take photos of the items as you pack them.

- Do you have insurance to cover lost or damaged baggage? It is a good thing to take with you when you travel. You may be covered under your homeowner's policy or a credit card. Check to see what you have and top up the coverage, if necessary, with a baggage insurance policy.

CHAPTER 50

How to Complain to the Canadian Transportation Agency

THE CANADIAN TRANSPORTATION Agency is a federal regulator that handles air travel complaints, among other things. It helps consumers who cannot get traction in resolving disputes with domestic or international airlines that operate in Canada.

Doron Horowitz, for example, had been trying to get a refund from British Airways for months. He booked a return trip from Toronto to London and Tel Aviv, but cancelled it after a Glasgow airport bombing backed up flights and the airline said that he could change or cancel his booking without a penalty.

Horowitz received a refund of $554.82, which covered the taxes paid, but he was out of pocket $2,500 on the remaining cost of the ticket. Since he was getting nowhere with British Airways, I suggested that he file a complaint with the CTA. Within two months, he got a credit for the amount owed to him.

Robert Sarner, another *Toronto Star* reader that I referred to the CTA, was fighting for compensation after Air Canada lost his wife's luggage. The bag was found later with damage and missing contents, but the airline refused to pay anything. His complaint took a year to resolve, but he did get an apology from Air Canada, along with an offer of the maximum compensation allowed ($1,800) and a $500 travel voucher.

Before you ask the CTA for help, you should give your airline a chance to resolve your complaint. You can find contact information for the major air carriers' customer service departments at the CTA website, www.otc-cta.gc.ca/eng/major-air-carriers-customer-service-departments.

In most cases, the agency tries to get airlines to follow their own rules, as written in their terms and conditions of carriage (or tariffs), and any international rules that may apply. Sometimes, the CTA reviews a rule to make sure that it is clear, reasonable and not unduly discriminatory. Gabor Lukacs, a crusader for airline passengers' rights, has succeeded in getting some airlines' baggage rules declared invalid.

Here are the types of air travel complaints the CTA will accept:

- **Baggage loss, damage or delay.** Airlines can set their own liability limits for travel within Canada. But they must observe rules (the Montreal and Warsaw Conventions) for round-trip travel originating in Canada and travel to and from Canada.

- **Flight disruptions.** Keep in mind that airlines do not guarantee their schedules. You may not get compensation for delays or costs incurred as a result of bad weather or mechanical breakdowns.

- **Tickets and reservations.** This includes lost tickets, expired tickets (most are valid for one year) and charges for issuing a new ticket. Reservations may be cancelled by an airline if the passenger does not respect the check-in time limits set by the carrier.

- **Denied boarding.** Also known as "bumping," this happens when an airline sells more seats on a plane than it has available and forces some passengers to take another flight.

- **Refusal to transport.** This happens when an airline refuses to let you board a plane or removes you from a plane because of something that you allegedly did or failed to do.

- **Passenger fares and charges.** The CTA can look at pricing by domestic airlines only on routes where there is no competition or very limited competition. It cannot look at complaints about the cost of international travel.

- **Cargo.** The CTA can look into cargo rates on domestic routes with little or no competition. On all routes, the terms and conditions for carrying cargo must be reasonable and not discriminatory.

- **Other issues.** The CTA can handle complaints about an airline's terms and conditions of carriage, such as those that may be considered unfair, unreasonable or discriminatory, or cases involving unaccompanied minors or animals.

The CTA also has a list of issues that it cannot deal with:

- The level and quality of customer service.

- Tour operators. You can complain about the air portion of a travel package purchased through a travel agent or tour operator. But complaints about the land portion of a package or service offered by a tour operator fall under provincial jurisdiction.

- Problems in airport terminals. You have to complain directly to the airport authority responsible for the airport. You can find links to Canadian airport authorities at www.tc.gc.ca/eng/programs/airports-caa-63.htm.

- Unfair competitive practices. You can send concerns about predatory pricing by air carriers and mergers or acquisitions that affect competition to the Competition Bureau, www.competitionbureau.gc.ca. An independent law enforcement agency, the Bureau has a basic operating assumption that "competition is good for both business and consumers."

- Loyalty programs. Some loyalty and frequent shopper programs, such as Aeroplan and Air Miles, are run by corporations that are independent of airlines. They are not under the CTA's jurisdiction. However, complaints about frequent flyer plans run by airlines can be sent to the CTA if the airline's response is unsatisfactory.

- Bilingual services. Canada's Official Languages Act applies only to Air Canada and its affiliates. You can address your complaints to the Commissioner of Official Languages, www.ocol-clo.gc.ca.

- Safety. Any complaints related to the safety on board an aircraft should be brought to the attention of Transport Canada, www.tc.gc.ca.

Since 2008, domestic airlines have been required by law to make their terms and conditions easily available to passengers at their offices and websites. You can complain to Transport Canada if the information is not displayed clearly.

CHAPTER 51

How to Enforce Your Airline Flight Rights

TRANSPORT CANADA enforces a code of conduct for Canada's airlines, called Flight Rights, which says that passengers have certain rights:

- **Information.** Airlines must make reasonable efforts to tell you about delays and schedule changes and, to the extent possible, the reason for the delay or change.

- **Overbooking or cancellation.** If your flight is overbooked or cancelled, the airline has to find you a seat on another flight or give you a refund of the unused portion of your ticket.

- **Punctuality.** If your flight is delayed more than four hours after the scheduled departure, the airline will give you a meal voucher. If a delay is more than eight hours and involves an overnight stay, the airline will pay for a hotel room and airport transfers if you did not start your travel at that airport.

- **Drinks and food on board.** If you are already on a plane when a delay occurs, the airline will offer you drinks and snacks. In a delay of more than 90 minutes, the airline will let you get off the plane until it is time to depart, if circumstances permit.

- **Luggage.** If your luggage does not arrive on the same flight that you do, the airline will deliver it to you as soon as possible. It will inform you of the status of the luggage and provide you with an overnight kit, if required.

Under the code of conduct, airlines are not responsible for bad weather or for acts of third parties, such as governments or air traffic control, airport authorities, security agencies, law enforcement or Customs and Immigration officials.

Ted Tjaden, a Toronto lawyer, flew to New York City over Christmas in December 2010. His return flight was cancelled because of a blizzard and rescheduled for the next day, forcing him to stay a night at a hotel in Newark, N.J. When he asked the airline to cover the cost, he was turned down.

"Perhaps not unfairly, in that situation when there is an act of God, the airline disclaims responsibility for putting up their passengers for the evening," he wrote at a legal blog, adding that he was just glad to have arrived home safely.

Flight Rights Canada's code of conduct says: "Airlines are legally obligated to maintain the highest standards of aviation safety and cannot be encouraged to fly when it is not safe to do so."

If you feel that an airline has not lived up to its legal rights, you can ask the CTA to mediate your complaint in an informal fashion. It will take all the relevant information from you (which can be done using an online complaint form) and give the airline a chance to respond. If you are unsatisfied after going through the informal process, you can launch a formal complaint with the agency.

The agency deals with about 500 to 700 air travel complaints a year. Most are resolved with facilitation or informal mediation in 30 days or less. Only a few complaints go to formal adjudication.

Allergies are a big focus for CTA. It takes the position that people with allergies can be considered to be people with disabilities if the allergies severely limit their access to the transportation network.

In 2010, the agency ordered Air Canada to accommodate passengers with nut allergies by creating a buffer zone in which it could serve only nut-free snacks and meals. In 2012, the agency ordered Air Canada, AC Jazz and WestJet Airlines to create a cat-free buffer zone of at least five rows when a person with a cat allergy gives at least 48 hours' advance notice of travel. Complaints from people with dog allergies were also being investigated.

Baggage liability is another issue that comes up in complaints. In 2010, the CTA found WestJet's limit too low. It ordered the airline to propose a higher limit, while allowing passengers to declare excess value for a reasonable extra fee. When WestJet's proposal was still too low, the CTA said it had to raise its liability limit to levels specified in the Montreal Convention (about $1,800). The case was precedent-setting in applying international rules to domestic travel.

So, if you have an air travel complaint that you cannot get resolved with an airline, contact the CTA at 1-888-222-2592. The e-mail address is info@otc-cta.gc.ca.

CHAPTER 52

How to Cross the Border with Your Travel Documents in Order

TO AVOID HASSLES when leaving Canada, make sure that you have the right travel documents. If your papers are not up to scratch or if you lack some papers that you are required to bring, you could be barred from crossing the border.

Here are some actual cases in which travellers have been stopped and barred entry to the United States or other countries:

- Your passport is worn out, soiled or water damaged.
- Your passport is close to its expiry date.
- You do not have the visa required to enter the country.
- You do not have a doctor's prescription or note for the drugs you packed in your suitcase or carry-on bag.

Tony Fasulo has a cautionary story about booking an Air Canada flight to Cancun, Mexico, with his family on December 27, 2011. When checking in at Pearson Airport in Toronto, his wife was told that she couldn't board the plane because her passport had water damage.

While her passport was worn out and did show some water damage, she had taken it with her on a flight to Mexico less than a year earlier. She had travelled from Canada to the U.S. a few times with no issues.

Fasulo was scrambling to get a new passport for his wife and make new travel arrangements for his family when he contacted me. He learned that the Mexican government had changed the rules about passports in the previous few months. However, Air Canada had not said anything or posted a message at its website.

WestJet has also refused to let passengers with water-stained passports fly to Mexico. A couple in London, Ont., who were denied boarding on a Mexico-bound flight, ended up going to Cuba a day later on WestJet, using the same damaged passport.

"We're really between a rock and a hard place here," said WestJet spokesman Robert Palmer. If people were allowed to fly to Mexico with damaged passports, they could be refused entry to the country and could have to fly back to Canada on the airline's dime. WestJet has warned that if you are travelling to Mexico, your passport must be perfect, with no rips, tears, missing corners or water damage. Store it properly. Keep it out of bags where it shares space with cosmetics, water bottles or shaving supplies. Buy a plastic sleeve that keeps it safe from damage.

Passport Canada recommends applying for a new passport if your current passport is damaged. "Travellers whose passports are damaged in any way could face significant delays or be denied entry at border crossings, or be denied boarding on flights," it says at its website, www.ppt.gc.ca. You can get an emergency renewal within 24 hours for a $70 fee by applying in person at a Passport Canada office.

It is better to replace a battered passport in advance of a trip than to make last-minute travel arrangements if you are barred from a flight. Do not expect compensation from the airline for your costs. Do not expect the Canadian Transportation Agency to reverse the decision. Under the law, airlines are not responsible for acts of third parties, such as customs and immigration officials.

Here are some other tips from Passport Canada:

- Renew early. Many countries require that your passport be valid for several months after your planned departure date from that country. To be safe, make sure that your passport is not close to its expiry date.

- Check travel reports for each country. Since the rules differ, you should check with the federal Department of Foreign Affairs and International Trade for local entry requirements, www.voyage.gc.ca.

- Scan page two of your passport and e-mail it to yourself. Or make a photocopy and carry it with you, separate from your passport. That way, you have identification if anything happens to your passport.

- Leave a copy of the second passport page with a trusted friend or relative who is not travelling with you.

- Keep your passport safe and not unattended in a suitcase, hotel room or vehicle. Carry it in a money belt, coat pocket, purse or backpack. You can also lock it in your hotel safe.

- Sign up with Registration of Canadians Abroad, which you can find at www.voyage.gc.ca. This free, confidential service will help the Government of Canada contact you and help you if there is an emergency (such as an earthquake or civil unrest) that you get caught up in while you are away.

- Each country sets its own visa requirements. Find out the rules before you go. A visa is an official document, usually stamped or glued inside a passport, giving permission from foreign authorities to enter a country.

Visas are issued by foreign government offices in Canada. You need to get one, if required, well in advance of your trip.

"You will almost certainly need a visa if you plan to remain in a foreign country for a longer period (usually more than 90 days)," says the foreign affairs and international trade website. "Before your departure, consult the travel reports for country-specific visa information."

When you are trying to figure out what documents you need for a trip, do not rely on a travel agent, tour company or airline agent for details. They are not experts in this area. Go right to the source, the federal foreign affairs department.

CHAPTER 53

What to Do with Your Prescription Drugs when You Travel

TAKING PRESCRIPTION MEDICATIONS with you can be a problem when visiting certain countries. You should keep your drugs in the original container and packed inside carry-on bags, says the foreign affairs department.

You are responsible for determining whether or not your medication is prohibited in some countries. It is smart to bring enough quantities with you to last longer than anticipated. As pharmacies sometimes run out of stock, you should also bring basic medicine, especially if you are travelling to outlying areas.

I once heard from a mother whose adult son was barred from entry when he went to Cuba in 2009 with a bunch of prescription pain killers. After a recent hip replacement, he was controlling the pain with a doctor's prescription for Percocet. Depending upon the degree of pain, he took up to three or four a day. So, he had a full supply of this drug.

At the Cuban airport, a customs officer asked to check his carry-on bag and saw the Percocet. (He had 60 tablets in his container.) He was told that it was an illegal drug and could not be brought into the country. Security guards immediately confiscated the entire amount.

He was told to take a cab to an international clinic, where he could get a prescription for painkillers. But the clinic did not have Percocet or anything comparable. He was given various papers by the doctor, all in Spanish, and felt confident that his Percocet would be returned to him.

When he returned to airport security, he showed the paperwork to the customs officer, but could not get back his Percocet. He had nothing to relieve his pain.

The young man felt that he could not stay without his medication. He flew back to Toronto the same day, paying $360 for airfare, plus $25 airport tax.

His angry mother wanted to recover all the costs, including the hotel lodgings, the trip to Havana and even the replacement medication. She was upset that the travel agency did not provide full disclosure. Though her son had bought travel insurance, he was unlikely to get a payout.

If the mother had checked the Cuba Tourist Board's website in advance, she would have found out that bringing narcotic drugs was prohibited, except for those for personal use accompanied by a doctor's prescription or letter.

Also, she could have checked the warnings at the federal foreign affairs website, headlined "Drugs and Travel." "Prescription drugs may be illegal in other countries," it points out.

Here are tips on travelling safely:

- Make sure the drugs you are carrying are legal and readily available in the country you plan to visit.

- Before you go, contact the embassy in Canada of the country you are visiting and confirm the status of your medication.

- Carry a copy of the original prescription, with both the generic and trade names of the drug, and a note from your doctor explaining why you are taking the medication.

CHAPTER 54

How to Avoid Getting in Trouble when Booking Hotels Online

ASIDE FROM AIRFARE, lodging is probably your greatest expense on a trip. You want a place to stay that is reasonably priced, and a hotel room that costs $200 a night can stretch your budget until it snaps.

To save money, you may be tempted to use travel websites—such as Hotwire and Priceline—that use an opaque pricing system. They help branded hotel chains advertise their inventory of unsold rooms at discounts of 50 per cent or more. There's one catch: The hotel's name will not be used.

This means you are flying blind when shopping for a hotel under the opaque system. Yes, you can choose the area where you want to stay. You can choose the star rating. You can choose the amenities, such as a swimming pool. But only after you make a reservation and pay up front do you find out where you will be staying.

Hotwire and Priceline give amazing deals for bargain-minded travelers who do not mind taking a gamble. Opaque deals are so popular that other websites are adding them. Expedia has "unpublished rate" hotels. Travelocity has "top secret hotels."

Here's the problem: star ratings are subjective and inconsistent. There are no established authorities.

"There's no high court of hotel stars, no international governing body," said Christopher Elliott, a U.S. consumer advocate and travel writer, www.elliott.org. "Any rating organization or online agency can arbitrarily award hotel stars (or take them away). There's no standard comparable to Europe's broadly accepted, quasi-official hotel and restaurant rating system."

So, how can you trust a website that does not reveal the hotel's name until after you book and pay in full? And how easy it is to get a refund?

A *Toronto Star* reader, Rosemary Frei, made an online booking with Expedia For TD, paying $300.99 for an unpublished rate hotel. (Expedia For TD is the preferred travel provider for TD cardholders to book travel and redeem points online.) But she panicked after seeing a bunch of negative reviews at TripAdvisor, a well-known website (www.tripadvisor.com), which said that the hotel had housekeeping problems, including bedbugs.

Frei decided to use her TD travel rewards to book another hotel that she could check out in advance. Then she tried to get her money back, arguing that the unpublished rate hotel did not deserve the 3.5-star rating that she relied on in making a reservation. Alas, she got nowhere with Expedia until I intervened on her behalf and got her a full refund.

When you use a website that offers huge discounts on unsold and unnamed hotel rooms, you do so at your own risk. The terms are clear. You pay in full, up front, and you do not get a refund. You get a message about no refunds just before you click to pay.

Mark Sousa was disappointed with Hotwire and tried to get a refund after booking a Las Vegas hotel with a 4-star rating. He felt that it did not live up to its billing after staying there. Later, he found that it had a 3.6-star rating at Hotels.com, an affiliated website.

"I believe the star ratings for sister companies Hotwire and Hotels.com should be in line," he said. But Hotwire said it benchmarked its ratings against other large travel sites. Expedia gave the hotel a 3.5-star rating. Travelocity and Orbitz gave it a 4-star rating (the same as Hotwire's).

"We don't take Hotels.com ratings into consideration when determining Hotwire star ratings," said spokeswoman Chelsea Jensen. "We remain confident the current 4.0-star rating of this property is an accurate reflection of its overall quality."

When using Hotwire or Priceline, you may even find that the hotel rates you get are not as good as the rates you could find on your own.

A reader asked me for help with Priceline. He had booked a 3-star upscale hotel in California, using the Name Your Own Price system, and saw a fine-print disclaimer that said: "Please note it is possible that the hotel you are booked in could be a Resort, which will meet or exceed the minimum qualifications of the star level you initially requested."

He went ahead and paid in full, despite his qualms about the fine print. Once he found out the hotel's name, he checked it out at TripAdvisor, where he found that one-third of the reviews were negative. Many people said that the hotel was not upscale.

Then, he went to the hotel's website and saw that he could pay $7 less per night if he booked the room directly by himself. Priceline refused to give him a refund, citing the contract terms, but paid him $20 to cover the difference in the room rates.

Can you trust the reviews you read online? Sean Shannon, Expedia's Canadian managing director, said that the reviews at its website are vetted and verified. The company tries to ensure that people have paid for a room in the hotel that they are reviewing.

As with all user-generated reviews, you have to read them carefully and look for trends. Your sense of skepticism should come into play if you see a few people raving about a hotel while most rate it as average or mediocre.

Before you use Priceline or Hotwire, you should check out the reviews posted online. At TripAdvisor, people often talk about the reasons that they chose a specific hotel and whether they used an opaque service. They try to assess how well the hotel's quality and service lived up to the ratings that it had been given.

CHAPTER 55

How to Avoid Being Denied a Refund on Unused Hotel Rooms

HERE ARE SOME TIPS on how to book low-priced hotel rooms through opaque websites, such as Priceline and Hotwire, which do not give the hotel's name until after you pay in full. The goal is to avoid running into problems that might lead you to cancel and be denied a refund:

- You will not have the chance to turn down specific hotels. So, if you have problems with a particular chain or if you need to be near public transportation, these websites probably are not for you.

- Opaque pricing works best in large cities where it is hard to find hotel rooms at low rates when you book them directly. If you pay $150 a night to stay at a motel, why not pay the same amount at Hotwire or Priceline and get a sell-off at a branded chain? The closer you book to your travel dates, the less you are likely to pay.

- Find the going rate for hotel rooms in the places where you plan to stay. Check Hotwire, which does not use Priceline's auction system, and see what it is asking for the same excess hotel rooms. Make that price your maximum bid and start lower.

- Priceline makes money if everyone overbids. But you can take advantage of a weakness in its system, since many people use Priceline and share information about their bids.

- Go to websites such as www.betterbidding.com and www.biddingtraveler. com to check out the winning bids from Priceline customers. You will get an idea of what kind of deal you can get and which hotels are on offer.

- Make a free re-bid. If your bid is not accepted, Priceline will let you bid again right away at a higher amount, if you change at least one of the requirements for your reservation. And if you have some spare time, you can bid again the next day without changing any of the requirements.

- Remember that there are no refunds, cancellations or transfers allowed. The opaque websites are known for being pretty strict about this rule. Be prepared to beg if you want a change.

- If all else fails, call the hotel directly and ask for the reservation department. It may be able to help you out, especially if you suggest that you will become a regular customer.

CHAPTER 56

How to Avoid Paying Medical Bills when Crossing the Border

BEFORE YOU TAKE A TRIP outside Canada, make sure that you are covered by travel medical insurance. This type of policy will reimburse you for emergency hospital and medical expenses that you incur while away.

Your provincial health care plan has limited coverage for such expenses, so you can end up with huge bills to pay if you are admitted to hospital or transported by air ambulance back to Canada.

You are taking a risk when you cross the border, even for a few hours, without supplementary medical insurance. If you get sick or injured while on a shopping trip to the United States, you could find that your treatment costs more than what your provincial plan will cover.

Here's a case history from Milan Korcok, a retired medical journalist who runs a consumer-oriented website on travel medical insurance, www.travelinsurancefile.com.

An Ontario woman went on a one-day trip to Buffalo, N. Y., to do some shopping and visit with her family for lunch. She had a stroke and was taken to a local hospital. Her condition was so precarious that she could not be driven to a hospital at home. After several days, she died.

"It was doubly shocking because she was only in her early sixties and always healthy," Korcok said. "And then came the bill from the hospital: over $150,000 for her family to pay. All of which could have been avoided by a simple transaction, done once a year, for less than the price she paid for her day of shopping."

For frequent border crossers, he advised, there is no substitute for an annual, multi-trip policy. You buy it once a year and you can take as many trips as you like out of the country, without having to fill out any more applications, make additional payments or even call your insurer to say that you are going. These multi-trip plans are the fastest-growing segment of the travel insurance market.

The Financial Services Commission of Ontario has an informative guide, *Shopping for Travel Medical Insurance,* posted at its website, www.fsco.ca.

Here are questions to ask before you leave the country:

- Do I have out-of-country medical insurance as a benefit at work? What is covered?

- Do I have out-of-country medical insurance as a benefit on my credit cards? What is covered?

- Do I need extra coverage from a travel agent, tour operator, airline or cruise company? How can I shop around for the best travel insurance deal at the lowest price?

- What is the maximum that each policy will pay above my province's medical insurance limits?

- Is there an age limit? Many out-of-country health plans offered as a workplace and credit card benefit end their coverage at age 65 or 70.

- How does the policy define a pre-existing condition? Will a pre-existing condition of mine affect my coverage?

- Are there any medical exclusions that apply to me?

- Will I have to pay a deductible? If so, how much?

- Does the policy contain a co-payment clause? What percentage of medical expenses will I have to pay?

- Will the insurance company pay the hospital or physician directly? Or will I have to pay the full amount myself, and then be reimbursed later by the company?

- Does the policy exclude any sports or activities I plan to do on my trip?

- Do I need approval from the company before seeking medical treatment?

- Does the company offering the policy provide a toll-free, 24-hour help line that I can call in an emergency?

- What if I want to stay away longer than originally planned? Can I extend my policy to cover me for the extra time I'm out of Canada and how do I make the necessary arrangements?

- What is the insurance company's procedure for handling complaints?

CHAPTER 57

How to Choose Trip Cancellation and Trip Interruption Insurance

YOU BOOK A VACATION, but you have to cancel at the last minute because of an illness or injury that makes it impossible to travel. You hope to get a refund because you paid with a credit card that has travel insurance benefits. However, you may not know which travel benefits you have on your credit cards until something goes wrong.

Many credit cards offer trip interruption insurance, which protects you from unexpected costs if you have an emergency while you are away. That is not what you need to be reimbursed for your prepaid travel arrangements. If you cancel before leaving, you must have a credit card that offers trip cancellation insurance.

It's easy to get confused. Most credit cards offer some travel benefits. Besides the two just mentioned, others may include:

- Flight delay
- Rental car protection
- Baggage delay or loss
- Hotel burglary insurance
- Common carrier accident (plane, boat, train, bus)
- Travel medical protection
- Roadside assistance

You probably choose credit cards by looking at the rewards or the interest rates. The extra features, such as travel benefits, may not catch your attention until something goes wrong. Then, you file a claim and learn, to your surprise, that your card has only trip interruption and not trip cancellation insurance.

What benefits do you have and what do you need? Luckily, there's an online tool that helps you do the legwork. The Credit Card Navigator—available at www.insureye.com and www.comparasave.com—lets you browse through a database of dozens of personal and business credit cards from major banks and retailers.

Suppose you are looking for trip cancellation coverage, which you think is more useful to you than trip interruption. You can pick credit cards and compare them to see whether they offer it or not.

Some credit cards, such as Capital One's no-fee Aspire Cash World MasterCard, have both trip cancellation and trip interruption coverage. Other credit cards, such as CIBC Aerogold Infinite Visa ($120 a year) and American Express Gold Rewards ($150 a year), have trip interruption only—and offer a trip cancellation option if you pay for it.

Some credit cards have no trip interruption or trip cancellation benefits, such as the no-fee President's Choice Financial MasterCard and BMO Air Miles MasterCard. Even the basic American Express card, which costs $55 a year, has no trip interruption or trip cancellation benefits.

I have heard many unhappy stories from consumers who had their claims denied. Some found out too late that they had the wrong travel insurance policy for their needs. Here are some examples:

- Ray Havelock took ill on a 17-day Caribbean cruise and flew home with his wife after five days. He had trip cancellation and baggage insurance, but did not have trip interruption insurance. He also had out-of-country medical insurance, but found that it would cover transportation home only if he was admitted to the hospital first. He was treated by a doctor on the cruise ship, so he had to pay for two return airfares ($1,100) and calls from the ship to make arrangements ($300). Meanwhile, he did not get a refund on the rest of the cruise.

- Lynn Samlal was taking a Caribbean cruise for her 20th anniversary with her husband. But the couple never left the ground in Toronto because their aircraft had mechanical problems. (Her travel agent had put them on a same-day flight in late December.) When she asked BMO

MasterCard to cover the $6,700 paid in advance, she found that she had only trip interruption coverage. She needed trip cancellation (alas, not offered on the card) to cover a delay before they went away.

- Sheila Gerlock was on a Caribbean cruise when a fellow passenger became ill. The ship was diverted to a hospital in a nearby port, forcing her and her husband to miss their flights back to Toronto. RBC Insurance wouldn't pay for new flights, even though its policy covered trip interruption. It said that a diversion caused by a passenger's illness was not a listed benefit. RBC reviewed the claim after Gerlock came to me and reimbursed her for $1,500. (The cruise line had kicked in a small amount for inconvenience.)

Sometimes you have the right travel insurance but you have to pay your own expenses for other reasons. Carole and Ken Brown's story should make you sit up and listen. The couple booked a trip to England, paying with travel rewards earned on an RBC Visa Infinite Avion card. They decided to cancel when Carole developed an eye problem that forced her eyelid nearly closed. Though they were covered for trip cancellation under a CARP insurance policy, their claim was denied.

The reason for denying the claim was that they paid for the flights with travel rewards, not cash. A free trip did not qualify for reimbursement, the insurer said. While the couple might have "paid" for the trip with their previous credit card transactions, they did not pay out any dollars for the flight. Thus, there was no loss.

Insurance companies use the same rationale in not covering flight or cruise cancellations when the carrier issues a voucher for future travel. Since the carrier is promising to make good, there is no loss.

The Browns' story has an epilogue. When CARP turned them down, they checked their RBC Avion card and found that they were covered only for trip interruption and flight delays, not for trip cancellation. They decided to change to another card, RBC Rewards Visa Preferred, which does offer trip cancellation coverage.

So, always check to see what insurance coverage you have on your credit cards, though your workplace or on any supplementary policy that you buy. You need trip cancellation and trip interruption coverage, not one or the other. And if you pay for a trip through reward points, be aware that you may not have an insurable claim.

CHAPTER 58

How to Fight Back when Your Trip Cancellation Claim is Denied

IF YOU CANCEL A TRIP before leaving, you can be denied coverage under a trip cancellation policy if you have a pre-existing medical condition that is not stable. The problem is that insurers have different ways of defining an unstable pre-existing condition.

For example, Bill Walker and Iris Lustig cancelled a trip to England when Iris had a flare-up of a chronic stomach ailment. Their claim was denied by the insurance company because Iris had a change in her medication shortly before the scheduled holiday. But her travel agent, Expedia, covered the flight cost as a goodwill gesture when I asked for help.

You can also be denied coverage if you cancel a trip because of the illness or death of a relative with an unstable pre-existing condition. Kathy Porritt booked a Florida trip with her sister, but cancelled when her sister was diagnosed with breast cancer and started chemotherapy right away. Her travel insurer, Manulife, refused to pay on the grounds that her sister's medical condition was not stable at the time that the trip was booked.

A stable medical condition, according to Manulife's definition, is one in which "there has been no admission to a hospital and/or you are not waiting results of further investigation for that medical condition."

Porritt went to small claims court to challenge the denial. She argued that her sister's cancer diagnosis came after the trip was booked.

"My sister had a mammogram, which showed only that she had a cyst," she told me. "It's frightening to think that every woman who has undergone a mammogram in recent months could be denied reimbursement for travel insurance if they are later diagnosed with breast cancer."

Going to small claims court was a successful tactic for Porritt, since Manulife paid the cost of all four cancelled trips a few months later without going to trial. A company spokesman said that when there are complex issues involved, such as a pre-existing condition, claims can require a detailed review and may take longer than average to settle.

So, here are some tips on choosing the right travel insurance:

- Check out the benefits offered by your employer and credit cards at a time when you are not booking a trip. Do your analysis well in advance of any travel arrangements.

- Top up your employer and credit card benefits, if incomplete, with an all-inclusive travel insurance policy.

- Try to deal with a travel agent or company that specializes in travel insurance. This is a complex field and needs expertise.

- You can compare the cost and features of travel insurance policies online at www.kanetix.ca, www.travelinsurancequotes.ca and www.travelinsurancehotline.com.

- Read the fine print and ask questions. You need to know what is covered and what is not covered.

- Fight back if your claim for compensation is denied. Escalate your complaint at the insurance company before appealing to the OmbudService for Life and Health Insurance (OLHI).

- If you buy your travel insurance from a bank, you can escalate to the ombudsman's office at the bank. Then, you can appeal to the Ombudsman for Banking Services and Investments (OBSI).

- If your complaint is about RBC or TD, your appeal must go to the ADR Chambers Banking Ombuds Office (ADRBO), www.bankingombuds.ca.

- If you strike out, consider hiring a lawyer to challenge the insurer. You can go to small claims court without a lawyer, but there's a limit on the amount of money you can get if you win your case.

CHAPTER 59

How to Avoid Losing the Travel Reward Points You Collected

YOU BELONG TO A LOYALTY PROGRAM, such as Aeroplan and Air Miles, which lets you collect travel reward points on your everyday purchases. You get extra points using a credit card or debit card linked to the program. One day, you hope to take a long trip to a faraway destination, subsidized by the points that you worked so hard to collect.

Do not wait too long to plan your dream vacation. Your reward points have a short shelf life and can disappear into thin air if not redeemed within a certain time period. Aeroplan points expire after seven years, while Air Miles points expire after five years.

Loyalty programs sound as if they are set up for the customer's benefit. But the real goal is to encourage you to shop until you drop, so that the retail partners make money. Loyalty programs also collect information about your shopping habits and sell it back to the retail partners to use in marketing campaigns.

To be profitable and successful, loyalty programs need active collectors. They want you to redeem your points for merchandise every few years and not hoard them for long periods, waiting for the right opportunity to cash them in at once. If you shop too little or too late, your points—and the trips you planned to take—could be history.

Always remember that reward points are not the same thing as money in the bank. They have no value, according to the terms and conditions of most plans, and they are worth only what a loyalty program says they are worth. A loyalty program can change the rules any time and can make the changes retroactive. You have no control. Get used to it.

Aeroplan began in 1984 as a frequent flyer program for Air Canada. But the airline ran into financial difficulty and decided to spin it off as a separate company (and potential money maker) in 2002. That was followed by an initial public offering of shares in June 2005. In 2012, the company changed its name to Aimia Inc. as part of its expansion beyond Canada and around the world.

The seven-year expiry date for Aeroplan reward points was announced in early 2007. (Many other loyalty programs already had expiry dates.) Members who joined before 2007 will see their points start to expire by January 1, 2014. Members who joined later will see their points expire seven years after they acquired them. Any points not redeemed in time will be removed from members' accounts on a monthly basis.

Also in 2007, Aeroplan made an immediate change designed to raise activity levels. Members lose all the points they have in their accounts if they do not collect or redeem any points during a one-year period. They are encouraged to get an Aeroplan-linked credit card or make regular purchases at retail partners, such as Esso, Home Hardware and Rexall/Pharma Plus, to avoid getting their points zapped.

Air Miles began in 1992 as an independent loyalty program, not owned by an airline. Unlike Aeroplan, Air Miles has a two-year activity rule. It waited until December 31, 2011, to implement a five-year expiry date. Members who earned Air Mile points before that date will have to redeem them by December 31, 2016.

"It was a decision we just had to make as a publicly traded company," said Neil Everett, Air Miles's chief marketing officer, referring to the company's parent firm, Alliance Data Systems Corp., which is listed on the New York Stock Exchange.

As publicly traded companies, both Air Miles and Aeroplan say that they face stricter accounting rules and more financial scrutiny. As a result, they can't keep carrying unused points on their balance sheets as a liability for years on end.

At least, Air Miles tried to offset the five-year expiration on points with a new benefit. Members can get immediate discounts at some retailers with any new points that they earn. Once they have 95 reward miles in a cash balance account, they can redeem them for $10 off their bill when they swipe their Air Miles card at the checkout.

Not everyone likes the instant redemption feature. Robb Engen, a *Toronto Star* personal finance blogger, noted that his favourite Air Miles reward was a $20 Shell fuel certificate. It used to cost 175 reward miles, but was changed to 190 reward miles as an instant redemption only. In his view, the Air Miles program was being devalued in the name of convenience.

Here are some tips on getting the most from Aeroplan and Air Miles:

- Read the loyalty program's terms and conditions. The importance of knowing the rules cannot be overemphasized.

- Think twice about using reward points for flights, since you still have to pay any taxes, fees and charges that the loyalty program wants to levy. Aeroplan and Air Miles kept fuel surcharges on North American flights after the airlines had dropped them.

- Pay cash for your flights and use your rewards points for upgrades to a higher status in the airplane or a better hotel room.

- If you travel with a partner, pay for one ticket on flights you want and book the second with reward points. You will find it easier to get accommodated, since reward seats sell out quickly.

- If possible, use your Aeroplan points to book flights on airlines other than Air Canada. You may use more points to pay for seats on Air Canada than on seats with its Star Alliance partners.

- Switch to credit cards linked to the Aeroplan or Air Miles program. They may offer a big sign-up bonus that can accelerate your points collection. Before you apply, get a free copy of your credit report. Make sure that your accounts are in good standing.

- Pay off your credit cards every month. Do not carry a balance, since the interest charges will outweigh the value of the points you collect. You might even lose your points if you fall behind on your payments.

- Check out the online mileage malls. At the Aeroplan online store (www.aeroplan.com/estore), you get one Aeroplan mile for each $1 you spend. At the Air Miles shopping mall (www.airmilesshops.ca), you get one Air Miles reward mile for every $20 that you spend.

- "Never go directly to a favourite retailer's website," says Brian Kelly, who runs The Points Guy website (www.thepointsguy.com). "Click through one of the online mileage malls and you will automatically get points for every dollar you spend. This adds up quickly."

- Hang on to your boarding passes. You will need them as evidence if an airline does not credit you with the reward miles you earned after taking a flight.

- Sign up for online access to your Aeroplan or Air Miles account. Check in each month to see what is going on. Make sure to collect or redeem Aeroplan miles once a year to avoid getting zapped by the activity rule. Watch your expiration dates carefully as well.

- Do not make big-ticket purchases just to collect points. Do not book flights when you can drive. You may have an obsession with acquiring points that is interfering with your financial judgment.

- Remember that loyalty programs make money for corporations by encouraging members to redeem their points for merchandise. The rules will change frequently if members do not shop enough and hoard the points.

- When you find the rules too restrictive and the constant changes too exasperating, just cancel your card and donate the points to your favourite charity. It could really use the help.

CHAPTER 60

How to Fight Back Against a Car Rental Company's Damage Claim

CAR RENTAL COMPANIES usually ask if you want to buy their "insurance." But what they are offering, at a steep cost of $15 to $35 a day, is not insurance but a collision damage waiver (CDW). This means that the rental company waives its right to collect a high deductible from you if the car is damaged.

You may already have collision coverage on rental cars through your own auto insurance policy. And if not, you may have a credit card that offers a type of zero-deductible collision coverage (comparable to CDW). If you rent a car with a gold card or platinum card, there is a better chance that you will have this coverage.

So, check your credit card benefits before renting a car. You can save a lot of money by declining the rental company's insurance. And consider applying for a card with this benefit if you do not have it.

Here's a story of a woman who bought the coverage and collided with fine-print exclusions that knocked out her claim (at first, anyway). Jacqueline Boone, a Canadian who lives in England, rented a car while in Toronto to attend a funeral. She had trouble reading the contract because of poor office lighting and asked if the collision damage waiver (at $25 a day) covered everything. She was told that it would.

Unfortunately, while driving out of an underground parking lot, she swerved to avoid a head-on collision with a car coming down the ramp and hit a wall. She called the company, Advantage Car & Truck Rentals, immediately to report the damage.

She thought she was fully covered, but when she checked her credit card online, she found an extra $5,558 in costs for the transaction.

Advantage later wrote to say that the repair costs were not covered because of a clause that excluded collisions with a stationary object—that is, a wall. She fought the company and won in small claims court, despite facing several lawyers on the other side.

She argued that the clause excluding collisions with stationary objects was not brought to her attention. She was not asked to initial it, as with other parts of the contract. And she cited another rental car case, where a judge said that the company had to take reasonable measures to bring onerous terms in a contract to the customer's attention.

Advantage launched an appeal, which was dismissed. The facts showed that Jacqueline did not consent to the exclusion, despite the clauses in the written contract, the judge said. The company was ordered to pay for the repair costs, plus $8,000 in court costs. However, the plaintiff was still out of pocket after covering her lawyer's bill and her trips back to Canada for court hearings.

Watch out for some other rental car whammies:

- Renting a car at an airport can cost you up to 50 per cent more than renting it in the city because of taxes and fees.

- Off-road driving can void your insurance and rental contract.

- Buying personal effects coverage for items stolen from the car is no bargain. Most valuables are excluded and the dollar cap is low.

- You may pay an inflated price for refuelling the car if you bring it back with less than a full tank of gas.

- You may pay an inflated price for repairing the car if you did not buy the rental company's collision damage coverage.

Jim Galpin, an Edmonton businessman, was presented with an outrageous bill to repair the windshield on a Budget car he had rented in Vancouver for two days. He was sent a picture showing a tiny chip in the windshield, with no cracks, below the driver's eye line. Then he was told that the entire windshield had to be replaced at a cost of $1,000 plus tax.

CBC News covered the man's plight as a warning to Vancouver visitors going to the Winter Olympics in 2010. It surveyed windshield repair outlets Crystal Glass and Speedy Auto Glass, which quoted a price of $25 to $60 to repair a small chip with no cracks. The repair shops then estimated that a windshield replacement on the rented Kia Rio should not cost more than $750.

The franchise manager encouraged him to call his credit card company to see if it would cover the bill, Galpin said. "I guess you know if you can put it through on your credit card and your insurance pays for it, then they figure the customer isn't out. But I just don't think that's right," he told the CBC's *Go Public* segment. Instead, he cancelled the credit card to stop Budget from putting the charge through.

To fight back against inflated damage claims, take your own pictures of the rental vehicle when you pick it up and when you drop it off. This is important if you drop off the car at a remote location or after hours. The photos can provide evidence that you are not responsible for the damage that the car rental company claims is your fault.

Galpin said he was told to return the car to the terminal when he finished with it and it would be picked up later. He thought this was a little strange. After dropping off the car, when he was about to fly out of Vancouver, he got a call informing him of the windshield damage.

When asked for a comment, the corporate head office of Avis Budget in the United States said that damage claims at Budget franchises were not the corporation's responsibility: "We cannot comment on their behalf, but we have put Mr. Galpin in touch with the licensee," it said.

If you want to check out a car rental company, search for the name and add "complaints" to your search. You can also go to travel review sites, such as TripAdvisor, to see what people are saying about a specific firm.

PART 5

fighting back against poor retail service

YOU GO INTO A STORE to buy an advertised special, but you cannot find the item you came in for. You cannot find an employee to help you.

Finally, you locate the advertised special and see that it is out of stock. Can you purchase it at a later date? Sorry, there is a limited quantity. You came too late and you are out of luck. You wasted your time tracking down the elusive deal and you have nothing to show for it.

Retail service in many Canadian stores ranges from mediocre to downright awful. You may recognize the details in the story that I just told you. You may have run into problems like that on a recent shopping trip. Canada has a few retailers with a reputation for excellence, such as Harry Rosen in men's clothing and Lee Valley Tools for hardware. But many stores seem to take little interest in satisfying customers and do not care if they buy anything or not.

Marketplace, the CBC TV show, did a hard-hitting show in January 2012 about poor customer service in retail chains. Almost half of the Canadians surveyed by Leger Marketing said they had a bad experience in the previous year. You can find the hour-long program at www.cbc.ca/marketplace.

Here were the top complaints about retail service in the survey:

- Long lineups at the checkout.
- Difficulty finding a salesperson.
- Rude or unfriendly salespeople.

When it came to after-sales service, the biggest beefs were:

- Having to fight too hard to resolve issues.
- Not getting their money back.
- Finding hidden limitations in return policies.

As part of its research, *Marketplace* hired mystery shoppers to test retail service across Canada and rate the major chains. The three chains that came out worst in the consumer surveys and tests were:

- Zellers was the number one offender with an F- grade.
- Canadian Tire received an F grade.
- Walmart received a D.

Surprisingly, many survey respondents also identified Walmart as the retail chain with the best customer service. It makes a good impression because it sells name-brand merchandise at discount prices. When you are saving a lot of money, you tend to overlook faults that you would criticize at stores selling the same brands at higher prices.

In this part of the book, I will look at how to fight back against poor service in retail stores. What if the advertised price was an error? Do you have any rights as a consumer when you are in such situations?

Retailers are tightening their return policies and introducing new limits. Many stores give refunds only if you bring back merchandise within a specific time period. Some deduct restocking fees from your refund. And some give no refunds at all, but only exchanges or store credits.

Long gone are the days of Eaton's, the Canadian department store known for its policy, "Goods satisfactory or money refunded." When the chain went bankrupt in 1999, Sears Canada took over some of the Eaton's stores. But Sears is much tougher about giving refunds when customers are not satisfied with the goods it sells.

In the *Marketplace* show, Zellers refused to give money back on a coffee maker that was sold as new, but was clearly used. There were scratches on the outside of the coffee maker and coffee grounds inside. Retailers that sell used items are supposed to label them as "open box" or "refurbished." Zellers failed to do that, but still insisted that a refund was not possible since the customer had missed the 60-day time limit. Only an exchange was allowed.

I often hear from readers who have a hard time getting help from retailers and manufacturers when they spend money on costly items that do not work properly—things like computers, smart phones, refrigerators, stoves, washing machines, dryers and other appliances.

When you feel that your complaints about quality and reliability are being ignored, you can use social media to put pressure on companies. Firms spend millions to promote their brands and do not want to see that image downgraded. They may be forced to fix or recall products when too many unhappy consumers make their voices heard.

Linwood Barclay, a well-known Toronto writer, was unhappy with his Sleep Country mattress purchase. The store refused to give him a refund or replacement, despite sagging springs in the first few months. In his letter to the chief executive, Christine Magee, he promised to talk about his sleepless nights to his thousands of Facebook friends. He now has a new Sleep Country mattress.

Canadian consumers tend to be more polite and tolerant of mistakes than U.S. consumers. We do not always speak up about practices that may be unfair or illegal. We settle for mediocrity.

If we want to see improved retail service, we have to raise our voices. Protest. Picket. Boycott. Otherwise, nothing will change.

CHAPTER 61

How to Fight Back when a Store Refuses to Give a Refund

RETAILERS ARE TIGHTENING the rules for refunds, exchanges and credits to cut costs. As a result, the policies can be a lot tougher than you realize. You cannot assume that you will get your money back, even when you bring back an item promptly with a receipt. An exchange or a credit may also be denied, depending on the circumstances of your purchase.

You should ask about a store's refund policy before you buy. It's your responsibility to learn the rules. Make it a habit to ask the question, but you have to avoid asking the wrong people.

Many readers tell me that they get false assurances from store staff when they ask about a refund. A young man named Matthew paid $418 for three pairs of jeans and a T-shirt and was told that he could return the clothing if it still had the tags on it. Only when he changed his mind two days later did he find out there were no cash refunds. The policy was printed in small type on the receipt and taped to a counter covered in merchandise.

A store manager or owner is probably your best source of information about the refund policy. An average employee may not know the rules or may give you an ambiguous answer (as in Matthew's case). Find out if the policy is written down anywhere. Look for signs in the store that say "no refunds." And if you are told that you can get your money back, ask the person to put it in writing.

As well, you should check a large retailer's website for information. You may be surprised to find that there are different refund policies for different items. The policy can be quite long and complicated.

Canadian Tire is a good example. Its rules depend on the type of merchandise that you buy, as you can see if you check the website (www.canadiantire.ca) under "Returns":

- You must return an item within 90 days in its original condition and packaging, with your receipt and Canadian Tire Money.

- Electronic items must be returned in 30 days (such as stereos, TVs, cameras and phones).

- Some products must be returned unopened (such as ink cartridges, memory cards, DVDs, CDs, books, mattresses and portable beds).

- Some products are not refundable (such as magazines, ammunition, fireworks, tinted paint and stain products and products cut to length or modified, plus clearance items).

- Gift cards cannot be returned or refunded. They must be redeemed for products or services.

- If a product is defective, the manufacturer's warranty will apply.

The last clause means that you can be denied a refund if you buy and try an appliance and find it unsatisfactory. One of my readers bought a grass trimmer at a Canadian Tire store. He brought it back after using it once and finding a smell of burning wire and smoke that made him concerned about safety. The store said he had to go the manufacturer for repairs under his warranty.

Here are some tips on how to get a refund or exchange when returning a product with a receipt, within the specified time limits:

- Ask to speak to the store manager. Talk about your history of shopping at the store and your future loyalty. Do not be angry or confrontational. Look for a solution that suits both sides.

- If you get nowhere at the store, contact the head office. Try to find someone who can bend the rules if you have a good reason for wanting a refund.

- Argue that the refund policy was not disclosed to you in advance. Stores should tell you if you can get your money back before you buy something, especially if you ask. It is not enough to disclose information on a receipt after you buy something.

- Opening a box should not be an excuse for denying you a refund or exchange. In many cases, you cannot check out a purchase to ensure that it suits you without removing the packaging.

- If one store says no, try another store in the same retail chain. Franchises such as Shoppers Drug Mart may have their own refund policies at each location.

- If your purchase is defective, demand a refund or exchange. Retailers have a duty to sell items that work properly and are fit for their intended purpose. They cannot evade that duty by sending you back to the manufacturer for repairs. Bring evidence to show that the merchandise is faulty.

- Keep your eye out for defects that show up in the first few weeks. If you wait too long to return an item as defective, you may find that a cash refund is out of the question.

Sometimes, a store will give a refund only if you fill out a form that asks for personal information. You can ask why the information is needed and how long it will be saved. You can ask to see the privacy policy. But at a certain point, you may have to give out a few facts about yourself in order to get your money back. (The information is used to identify customer abuse patterns, such as the returning of stolen items.)

Stores often deduct a "restocking fee" from your refund to pay for the administrative work in putting an item back on their shelves. Ranging from 10 to 25 per cent of the purchase cost, plus sales taxes, restocking fees tend to be applied to larger purchases.

"It is almost impossible to sell some items as new once they have been taken out of their original packaging," said Sears Canada spokesman Vincent Power. "Customers are skeptical of open boxes. If they buy something as 'new,' then it needs to be new.

"With a used snow blower, we would not sell it to another customer as new. Therefore, we would have to take a loss on the item before selling it to a customer again, plus have a service check done on it to ensure that it is in proper working condition to be resold and empty it completely of gas for shipping back to a store," Power said.

In my view, stores that charge a restocking fee are making a decision to penalize customers who return items, instead of raising prices across the board and penalizing everyone. They should warn you that you may not get a full refund when you return something.

If you are hit with a restocking fee, you can argue that you did not see any information at the checkout desk. Moreover, no one brought this to your attention when you were paying for your purchase. Disclosure is not really disclosure if it occurs after the fact, such as on a receipt, rather than at a time when it can influence your purchase decision.

CHAPTER 62

How to Get Your Money Back when You Pay with Your Credit Card

THERE IS AN ADVANTAGE to using a credit card for a major purchase. If you want to return the item and you cannot get a refund from the store, you can ask the credit card issuer to reverse the transaction. This gives more protection than using cash, cheque or debit cards (as long as you pay your credit card balance each month and avoid interest fees).

When you use a Visa, MasterCard or American Express card, you have a zero liability guarantee against unauthorized use of your credit card. The guarantee applies to purchases made in a store, by mail and telephone or on the Internet. In general, you are not held responsible for credit card charges that you did not agree to accept.

Suppose you ordered a carpet, but the store went bankrupt before delivery. If you paid with a credit card, you could get back your deposit. But if you paid with cash, cheque or a debit card, your deposit would most likely disappear.

Credit card issuers have deadlines for refunds. Check the fine print on your statement. In general, when disputing a transaction, you have to do it within 60 to 90 days of making the transaction or having the statement mailed to you. But there is an exception: if a store fails to send merchandise that you ordered, you can dispute the charge within 60 to 90 days of the latest anticipated delivery date.

One of my readers put down a $450 deposit for custom-made furniture and was still waiting for his order when the store went out of business six months later. His credit card company turned down a refund, saying that the 90-day period for disputes was over.

The reader succeeded in recovering his $450 deposit because he had the right paperwork—an e-mail from the store, promising to send his furniture by May 1. And since he was disputing the transaction in June, he was still within the 90-day period.

To protect yourself, try to use a credit card when ordering something to be delivered in the future. Then, you can ask the credit card company for a refund. If you are turned down because you missed the deadline, go through your e-mails and receipts to find the latest delivery date. (And always ask a store to put delivery dates into writing.)

Besides deadlines, you may find other limits on your right to dispute a credit card charge under the zero liability guarantee. For example, MasterCard Canada's website mentions three conditions: (1) Your account must be in good standing. (2) You must have exercised reasonable care in safeguarding your card. (3) You cannot have reported two or more unauthorized events in the past 12 months.

MasterCard is not alone in limiting the number of times that you can ask to reverse unauthorized payments. Visa and American Express have a similar position (even if unwritten). If you contact a credit card issuer each month to complain about recurring payments, you may be told to contact the retailer directly.

Recurring payments occur when you sign a contract with a fitness club, a home maintenance company or a telecom provider (among others) and change your mind later. Frustrated with being locked into a contract that you no longer want, you decide to launch a dispute with your credit card company.

Credit card companies may reverse recurring payments once or twice. But they refuse to block them each month, because they do not want to get involved in contract disputes between a retailer and a customer. They tell you to work things out with the company that signed you up to a contract. The zero liability guarantee does not apply in this case.

One of my readers, Jamie, got into a recurring payment dispute online. She ordered a free tooth-whitening product after finding that a Facebook friend loved it (her friend's account was hacked). She agreed to give her credit card number to cover shipping costs, but did not read all the fine print.

Later, she went on live chat to ask the company why the shipping fee was $11.90, instead of the advertised $1.95. That is when she learned that she was on the hook for monthly shipments of the tooth whitening product at $85 apiece (plus tax).

"My credit card company is supportive, but is not willing to do much," Jamie told me. "They made it clear to me that I was still responsible for the charge, because I had agreed to the terms and conditions prior to completing the sale."

The scam is called continuity billing, "an appropriate term because if you fall for it, you will experience a continuity of regret," says CreditCards.com. "The remorse continues because your credit card is billed each month for generally worthless services you were tricked into authorizing."

Cancelling a credit card can stop monthly payments that you do not want to continue. But the tactic is not foolproof. Some billers have the ability to track you down and put through charges on a new credit card.

Suppose you ask your credit card company to reverse a transaction. Should you notify the retailer whose charge you are disputing? I think it is a good idea to do so.

A credit card refund backfired for my readers Dana and Brian McPhail, who put down a $2,200 deposit on a custom-made door that was to be delivered in eight to ten weeks. Still waiting after six months and getting no response from the retailer, they asked the credit card company to return the deposit.

The retailer was unhappy to see the transaction reversed and filed a small claims court suit for $15,000 in damages. It also put a $12,000 lien on their house, saying that the contract specified no refunds for delays beyond its control. The door finally arrived a few days after the couple got their credit card refund.

Be aware that the zero liability guarantee for unauthorized transactions may not apply in cases where your personal identification number (PIN) is used with the credit card to make a purchase. TD Canada Trust told customers in July 2012 that it was changing its contract language to say that a purchase made with the customer's PIN was considered to be an authorized transaction.

While TD was the first to draw cardholders' attention to the provision, the other big banks have all updated their cardholder agreements in a similar way. They want you to be responsible for safeguarding your PIN. And if they think you are not doing it, they will penalize you.

Here is my advice:

- Give your credit card information only to companies that you know and trust.

- Read the offers carefully. Check the agreement and look for warnings or disclaimers. Print out the online information before clicking "Yes" to what looks like a great deal.

- Make sure that no one else but you can discover or use your PIN. Keep it secure. Never use a series of numbers that a fraudster could detect (birthdates, addresses, etc.).

- Do not agree to a monthly subscription, since you can lose your protection against unauthorized transactions.

- Read your monthly statement and call the company to question any charge that you do not recognize.

CHAPTER 63

How to Return a Purchase That You Make Online

SHOPPING ON THE INTERNET can save money. You may find that some items are much cheaper than at a bricks-and-mortar store, even after you pay the shipping costs, but the savings can disappear if you have to return your purchase.

Online-only retailers often ask you to pay the shipping costs to send back an unwanted item. For example, check the return policy of Amazon.ca, which sells books, music and other products online.

If the return is the result of our error, we'll pay the return shipping costs, says Amazon. If the return is not the result of our error, the shipping cost of that returned item will be deducted from your refund. The amount deducted will be the equivalent of our standard shipping costs for that item.

You may be better off patronizing retailers (such as Indigo Books, Best Buy, Future Shop and Home Depot) that sell online and in their stores. You can buy items at discount prices at their websites, but if you have to return a purchase, you can drop it off at any of their stores.

Adam Goodman, a Moneyville blogger, bought a Bluetooth headset at 50 per cent off from an online retailer. The device stopped working just a few hours after it was delivered. The manufacturer said it was DOA—defective on arrival—and was actually a refurbished unit sold by an unauthorized retailer.

A quick call to the retailer resulted in a refund, Goodman said, but he had to contact the retailer two more times to waive the shipping fee and the restocking fee. This experience taught him a few things:

- Avoid deals that sound too good to be true. When he went back to the retailer's website, he saw many reviews that talked about the Bluetooth headset being DOA. "Too bad those reviews weren't available when my order was placed," he said.

- If you want to ensure you get a functioning product, buy from an authorized retailer.

- Read the fine print. Goodman did not know all the details. Luckily, he bought from an online store with a good refund policy. He could have been stuck with a useless piece of plastic.

- Many retailers rely on the consumer's unwillingness to complain. Though he did get a refund, he had to call the retailer three times to get all the fees waived. Whenever returning an item, especially for a warranty issue, insist that the retailer waive any shipping or restocking fees.

Even bricks-and-mortar retailers may have special rules for returns when you buy online. For example, you cannot return major appliances bought at HomeDepot.ca. You have to inspect them thoroughly at the time of delivery, and if you are not satisfied, you have to refuse them before signing the delivery receipt. Any product defects or damages you find must be reported within 48 hours of delivery.

Reading the fine print could have helped Agatha Filion avoid a disaster. She bought a Samsung TV online at Best Buy months before a move. Her husband was asked to check its condition on delivery and did so. The TV was wrapped in plastic and did not appear damaged. They left it in the box from May to November. When they finally took it out and turned it on, they found that the screen was broken.

Samsung refused to cover the damage under warranty. It had a policy that a customer had to report any damage within 48 hours of delivery. Filion said she bought the TV because the deal was too good to resist and had no need for it until moving to a new house. Since repairs would cost more than the TV was worth, Best Buy gave her a $250 gift card to use for a replacement.

Always check the return policy with online purchases, since it may differ from the return policy for items bought in the store. Inspect major appliances when they are delivered or within the next day or two. Report any damage right away. If you leave an appliance in a box, you will be blamed for any subsequent damage.

Ordering flowers from an online retailer can lead to problems if the arrangement shows up late or wilted. Look for online reviews of the retailer's customer service. You want to be able to escalate a complaint if the floral delivery does not meet your expectations.

Remember that if an online retailer refuses to give your money back, you can ask your credit card issuer for a refund. Visa, MasterCard and American Express have a zero liability policy for unauthorized use of your credit card. This applies to a failure to deliver what was promised.

Credit card companies introduced zero liability protection as a way to make consumers feel comfortable about buying on the Internet. If you have a choice of payment methods, using a credit card for purchases can provide more safety. However, there is no guarantee that you will get a refund, especially if you do not complain within a tight time limit.

CHAPTER 64

How to Avoid Getting into Trouble with Online Purchases

ONLINE PURCHASES are more common than they were, but you have to protect yourself. Which retailers can you deal with safely? Do they have good reviews? Can you find any complaints? How do you know that they are selling genuine goods, not fakes? Caution is needed, since you cannot visit the company premises or meet the staff face to face.

The Canadian Anti-Fraud Centre tracks the latest trends in online scams and deceptions at www.antifraudcentre.ca. This is the place to go when you get a call from someone who says they work for Microsoft and wants to protect your computer from crashing. Another popular scam urges you to wire money overseas to help a friend or family member who is in jail or who cannot return home because of a stolen passport.

There are other traps that can ensnare the unwitting buyer. You may fail to read the small print and get stuck with a subscription for a monthly purchase of vitamins or cosmetics, rather than the free sample that you thought you had ordered. You may think you are buying tickets for a concert or sports event directly from the box office. Instead, you find out after you paid that your order was processed by a reseller that charged two or three times more money for the ticket than the listed price.

Every time a fraudulent scheme is killed off, a new one crops up. It's like Whac-a-Mole, the carnival game. You will never win against the pesky critters. So, take precautions. Here is how to do it:

- Arm yourself against fraud, which is always present and more visible than ever in this interconnected world.

- Do not trust strangers who approach you out of the blue to help. Hang up the phone. Kill the e-mails. If they offer a service that you want and need, you can find it elsewhere on your own.

- Contact the companies that are supposedly contacting you to warn you that your identity has been compromised. Ask them if the threat is real or a mistake.

- Never let up your guard. When you get an offer that sounds extremely enticing, assume that it is a scam unless you can prove otherwise.

- Read the *Little Black Book of Scams*, a 30-page online publication by the federal Competition Bureau, www.competitionbureau.gc.ca.

  Here are a few more tips for online buying:

- Shop only with trusted retailers that you have investigated for customer service excellence.

- Check the retailer's return and delivery policies, as well as the privacy policy.

- Use a secure browser when shopping online. You will see the locked padlock icon and the letter "s" following "http" in the website address.

- Keep copies of all online transaction documents. Screenshots can also be helpful.

- Never send payment or credit card information through e-mail, since it is not secure.

- Use a credit card that offers zero liability for fraud and unauthorized use.

CHAPTER 65

How to Fight Back Against Online Fraud

By David Malamed

David Malamed is a partner in forensic accounting at Grant Thornton LLP in Toronto. He is also **CAmagazine's** *technical editor for fraud.*

ONLINE FRAUD is a real risk. Remote transactions through the anonymity of the Internet have increased your susceptibility to becoming a victim.

Here are tips that will help you prevent it from happening:

- Remember that there is no such thing as easy money with little risk and work effort. It's basic, but you need to remember this fact when considering easy money offers: If it seems too good to be true, it probably is.

- Conduct your own due diligence before doing business with an organization. Verify the contact details (such as physical addresses and phone numbers). Don't do business with organizations that will not freely provide you with their details.

- Make sure a website is secure before you send personal information. For example, Internet Explorer uses a locked padlock to show that a site is secure. All online transactions need to be made over secure websites. Part of your due diligence is identifying the safest way to pay for purchases.

- You need to have some degree of recourse if there is a dispute. So, do not send cash or use wire transfers when paying for online goods, services or auction items.

- Antivirus and anti-spyware software is not a catch-all solution. The programs are only as good as what has already been identified about the new software that fraudsters continually develop.

- Make sure that your software is up to date and installed properly. Check that it is turned on.

- Be cautious about what you download, what e-mail attachments you choose to open and what websites you visit.

- Your bank will not contact you by e-mail asking for account information or verification. If you receive an e-mail request from a financial institution, call them directly (use the phone number on the back of your bank or credit card) to find out if they need something verified or updated.

CHAPTER 66

How to Fight Back when You Find a Pricing Error

MY READERS OFTEN ask me about pricing errors. Does a retailer have to honour a published price if it is incorrect? This question comes up when stores advertise deals that seem too good to be true and then apologize for making a mistake.

Under the federal Competition Act, companies cannot sell a product at a price that is higher than the advertised price. However, this provision does not apply if the advertised price was a mistake and was corrected immediately.

Retailers often make errors, especially when they have online sales. So, if you pay for a sale item and find later that you cannot get the item at the advertised price, you should ask the retailer for compensation. You are disappointed and you want to feel that your business is valued, even if this particular transaction is not completed.

For example, Tomas Didi saw an item advertised at Best Buy's website, a Nintendo Wii priced at $199.99 in a sale that ended on December 24. But when he tried to buy the video game console at a Best Buy store on December 18, he was told the price had gone back to $209.99.

Best Buy had lowered the price in reaction to a competitor that was selling the Nintendo Wii at $199.99, said spokeswoman Shannon Kidd. When the competitor stopped selling it at that price, Best Buy did, too. "It's rare when that happens," she said, referring to the sale's premature end.

Didi received an e-mail after he complained to the *Star*, apologizing for his frustration and inconvenience and offering to let him buy the Nintendo Wii at $199.99.

Another reader, Garvin Hoo Sang, found a pricing error at Future Shop's website during an after-hours sale. A high-definition TV with a 52-inch screen was reduced to $1,999.99, but was showing a price of $1,199.99 in the first 90 minutes of the sale.

He bought the TV at the incorrect lower price and received e-mails from Future Shop on the same day, saying that his order was confirmed and processed. Five days later, he got another e-mail saying that his order had been cancelled because of a pricing error.

When he protested, and I asked Future Shop to help, he was given a $100 gift card for being a loyal customer. The retail chain processes hundreds of thousands of transactions, Kidd said. "We're incredibly diligent at proofreading, but there's an input by a human at some point." That human input can lead to errors, which are not detected until after an advertisement is published.

Future Shop had another embarrassment with an advertised special on Polk Audio Tower speakers, featured at $349.99 in the store's online Boxing Day sale in 2011. Alas, the online price was incorrect and should have been $699.99 per pair.

About 150 customers ordered online, expecting a pair of speakers. But they actually paid $349.99 for a single unit. Many people wrote to me about the retailer's clumsy attempts to make good on its error.

Future Shop said it would honour the price mistakenly advertised, but it could not supply a second speaker to customers who wanted one because they were out of stock. It promised to give refunds to anyone who asked and a $150 gift card to use for online purchases.

Stores such as Future Shop recognize that when a price is incorrect, customers are inconvenienced. Even if they get their money back, they lose out on a chance to buy the same product at another retailer's sale. I'm talking about the opportunity costs involved with a transaction that cannot be completed because of a pricing error. A refund is not enough to compensate you for missing the chance to get the low-priced deal you wanted elsewhere. So, you should always ask for more.

Here are other tips on fighting back when you find a price error:

• Tell the retailer that you will file a complaint with the federal Competition Bureau (www.competitionbureau.gc.ca), which looks into misleading advertising. You can do so if the price error was not corrected right away, but kept being published for a few days.

- Check into the scanner price accuracy code adopted by many retailers. It says that when the scanned price of an item without a price tag is higher than the shelf price, you are entitled to receive the item free if it is worth less than $10, or receive a $10 reduction for more expensive items. You can find information on the voluntary code at the Competition Bureau's website.

- Take screenshots of sale prices and confirmation orders from an online retailer. They can be useful evidence when you find that you cannot buy the item you want at the price you want because of a mistake that has been corrected.

CHAPTER 67

How to Fight Back Against Automatic Renewals

COMPANIES OFTEN SELL you a service that lasts for a specific time, such as one year, but can be renewed automatically. Since they have your payment information on file, they can put through another charge for the service when the initial term expires. It is up to you to know when this might happen and try to stop it.

For example, if you have a computer, you may use antivirus software from McAfee or Symantec. These companies tend to renew your subscription automatically each year unless you cancel within the first 60 days.

Doug Kinsman did not realize his first purchase of McAfee software would lead to endless renewals. He was unhappy to learn that he was charged $69.99 for a one-year renewal when the company offered the same thing for $34.99 at its own website.

An e-mailed renewal notice caught his attention and made him angry enough to ask his credit card issuer to reverse the transaction. But he did not get anywhere since the information was disclosed to customers, albeit in small print.

You have to click "I accept" to McAfee's auto-renewal provision before your online purchase is completed. Among 23 terms and conditions is one that says your subscription will be automatically renewed—and charged to the account you have provided—before your current term expires. The charge goes through unless you say in advance that you do not want to renew.

"McAfee wants to ensure our customers are safe from online threats and cybercriminals," said spokeswoman Cassie Prosper. "Auto-renewal guarantees that consumers will not have a lapse in security. Even a short, unintentional lapse could result in irreversible damage or irretrievable data loss."

Many companies—including fitness clubs, car and home insurance providers, lawn care companies, furnace contractors and newspaper or magazine publishers—also renew your service automatically. They can do so without advance notice because of an agreement you made at the beginning. They say it is for your convenience, so that you will not lose protection through an accidental oversight.

The downside is that it is harder to enjoy discount offers as an auto-renewal subscriber. You may be better off cancelling your contract before it expires and starting over again. Then, you can shop around for the best prices.

McAfee says on its website that all subscriptions are automatically renewed "at the then-current price for the service, which excludes promotional and discount pricing." As Kinsman was upset to find, this meant that the software price was higher for long-time loyal customers than for new customers.

In his view, McAfee should give existing subscribers the best available current rate. He also wanted to see any conditions that might cost you more in bold print at the top of a contract or enrolment form.

When I bought a $39.99 antivirus program to check the disclosure, I did not see anything to warn me, except in the five-page license agreement that I had to click before paying. My confirmation receipt, sent by e-mail, was silent about the auto-renewal.

Here are some tips to fight back against the automatic renewal of services:

- Make a note to remind yourself of the expiry date. Keep it in a place where you can find it easily. This may be the only record of your enrolment.

- Remember that you may not be given any advance notification of the renewal. And if you want to get out, you may have only a month or two after the renewal to cancel without penalty.

- You can ask a company to ask for permission before renewing your service, but not all companies will do this. They prefer to renew your contract and wait for you to cancel it.

- Once they have your credit card number on file, companies can continue renewing their services one year after another. Even *Consumer Reports*, the well-known magazine, operates this way.

- Cancel the credit card used for the transaction. This can help if you find yourself stuck in a one-year contract with no opportunity to cancel for another 10 months. But be aware that some billers can get hold of your new credit card information and keep putting through the charges.

- Be skeptical when companies insist on credit card payments as a condition of providing a service. Ask them if they will take cash, cheques or money orders instead.

- Before giving out your credit card number, ask a company if it uses automatic renewal. Read the small print carefully to see what unfair conditions might await you there.

- Look for alternatives to auto-renewals. In a competitive market, you should be able to find companies that will bill you in advance and only provide a service after you make your payments.

CHAPTER 68

How to Avoid Losing Money on a Gym Membership

By Nicholas Ross

Nicholas Ross is the proprietor of Prevail Business Consulting in Toronto. A long-time advocate of greater consumer protection, he pursued a complaint about questionable business practices in the fitness industry with provincial ministries and law enforcement. He concluded that the only way to produce a satisfactory outcome is to contact the media.

ACQUIRING A GYM MEMBERSHIP should be easy, but there are few businesses that generate customer complaints so consistently. Here are some precautions you can take to avoid being cheated:

- Research gyms online.
- Combine their name with key words such as "fraud" and "scam." Finding a lot of complaints, especially if they go back several years, should raise suspicions. You can simultaneously determine what a reasonable monthly fee is.

    When you visit the gym:

- Don't sign up on your first visit.
- Bring a friend to whisk you out the door when the salesperson has finished their pitch.

- Don't reveal your title or income. Sales personnel can often negotiate with you on prices, but they are unlikely to offer a good deal if you sound prosperous.

- Don't commit to personal training at the outset. Observe the trainers in action and speak with clients. Trainers often do not have formal credentials, so their ability to train people safely is uncertain.

- Pay dues with post-dated cheques. Your post-dated cheques should be drawn on a bank account dedicated solely to gym payments. This protects your main account from fraud. Stories about money being siphoned from customers' accounts are too numerous to ignore. If a gym will not accept post-dated cheques, it's probably better to find a gym that does.

- Think twice about paying cash up front for a year. This helps avert fraud, but if the gym folds, you are unlikely to get anything back.

- Never use a credit card for payments. Some unscrupulous gyms put through extra charges on your credit card during the membership or months or even years afterward. They find ways around blocks that credit card companies put in place to prevent unauthorized charges.

- Never accept a verbal agreement. Make sure any extras or special terms are written on the contract and initialled. And make sure you get a copy of the contract you sign.

- Do not assume your contract expires at 12 months. Most gyms roll memberships over unless a member takes specific steps to cancel.

   When cancelling your membership:

- Always remember to communicate in writing and retain copies.

- Read the gym's cancellation requirements, especially with respect to timing.

- If you paid with a credit card, pay it off and cancel it. Refrain from getting another card from the same issuer. Unscrupulous gym owners have been known to obtain new numbers.

- E-mail is not without its drawbacks. Many e-mail systems do not provide "delivery" or "opened" receipts, so recipients can deny knowledge of them.

- Instead, send a fax to the manager of the club and to the head office. Getting the right names may take a little persistence.

- A major benefit of this approach is that you receive a hard copy transmission verification report that proves the fax went through, a date and time and an image of the first page sent in reduced size.

- The fax may be the definitive proof that you need when dealing with the gym or your bank. So don't lose it!

CHAPTER 69

How to Decide on Getting an Extended Warranty

WHEN YOU BUY an appliance or electronic product, the store often gives you a strong pitch to buy an extended warranty to cover repairs for a few years. Do you go for the warranty? Or do you decline?

Here is how to play the game so that you get the protection you need without being overcharged:

- Check your credit card coverage. Many cards offer a purchase protection plan that doubles the warranty you get from the manufacturer, up to one year, when you charge the full price to the card. Even if you pay an annual fee for the card, it may be cheaper than buying the store's extended warranty.

- What coverage do you get with the extended warranty? And who administers it? Ask for a copy of the warranty contract and read its terms before saying yes or no. Keep in mind that any insurance policy has loopholes and exclusions. It's better to find out in advance, rather than wait until you make a claim.

- When does the extended warranty coverage kick in? Does it start with your purchase? You may find the retailer's warranty overlaps with the manufacturer's warranty in the first year. You need to know about this overlapping coverage.

- Do you want to get a retailer's warranty anyway? It might offer extra benefits, such as Future Shop's and Best Buy's no-lemon guarantee and 60-day repair guarantee. You might get a product replaced under the store's warranty when a manufacturer refuses to do so.

- Check the cost of the product you buy and the cost to replace it. An extended warranty can be worthwhile on an expensive item that you hope to keep for a long time. It makes less sense for low-cost items, when the technology is changing quickly and the replacement cost can drop significantly after a few years.

- Remember that extended warranties are very profitable for retailers. Much of the cost is for marketing and very few people make claims. So, negotiate on the price and see if the store will throw in the warranty for free if you are making a large purchase.

- Remember, too, that a serious product safety or quality issue supersedes a warranty. It does not matter if you have passed the one-year time limit. The manufacturer still has to fix the problem. The sale of goods act in every province says that products must be fit and suitable for the purpose for which they are intended.

So, why do retailers' and manufacturers' warranties overlap? Is it a marketing ploy to make store warranties appear more attractive?

Jack and Liz Le Blanc bought an Apple iPad at Future Shop. They paid $109 for a two-year store warranty that covered them from the purchase date. When the iPad didn't work properly, Liz brought it back to the store.

"She was told it was the manufacturer's problem because the unit was less than a year old," Jack says. "No one at Future Shop was able to say what the first year of the company's insurance actually covered."

The Le Blancs will get their iPad replaced by Apple, but they feel that Future Shop's warranties promise more than they deliver.

"You don't get to look at the fine print until after your purchase," Jack points out. "In truth, the manufacturer's warranty covers any problems in the first year and the insurance policy you've bought is only good if the manufacturer does not fix or replace it. This is simply not going to happen with any reputable manufacturer."

Future Shop spokeswoman Shannon Kidd said the store's warranty offers additional benefits during the first year of ownership. There is a "no-lemon guarantee," which means that you get a free replacement if your product is repaired three times and it requires a fourth repair for the same issue. There's also a guarantee of getting a product replaced if it takes longer than 60 days to repair.

"Each manufacturer has a different agreement that stipulates how we handle repairs or replacements during the first year," Kidd says. "In this case, the manufacturer replaced the item, which is the best outcome for the customer. The extended warranty still covers the product for the balance of the contract.

"If the manufacturer had not agreed to replace the product, then Future Shop would have determined what was best for the customer—most likely a replacement under the extended warranty."

With the complexity of major appliances and their habit of breaking after the first year, you may decide to opt for the extra coverage. But if you do buy a store's warranty, make sure you understand how it differs from the manufacturer's warranty and which years it covers. Do you want an overlap?

In some cases, appliance manufacturers or retailers will pay for repairs even after the one-year warranty has passed. I know this happens since I was able to get a free repair on my GE oven, barely three years old.

One day, I closed the oven and heard a "thunk." I saw pieces of glass fall from the door, landing in the drawer below. I was shocked to see my glass door shatter, since I did not use the oven every day and I had never used the self-cleaning feature (which boosts the temperature).

Then, I did an Internet search and came up with other instances of shattered glass on other brands of ovens. In response to news stories, Sears Canada said it would give free inspections to anyone who was concerned about the problem. It would also do repairs free of charge.

Once I saw that Sears was covering it, I sent a message to GE Appliances on Twitter. It tweeted back within minutes, offering to help. And by the next day, I knew that I would get a free door repair as well.

If you want the manufacturer to help after the short warranty period, consider patronizing a smaller store when buying major appliances and electronics products. Get to know the owners and managers. Then, enlist their support when you are fighting with the manufacturer. That can be an effective tool to get free repairs or replacements.

Consumer Reports has always advised readers not to buy extended warranties, with two exceptions: AppleCare for Macintosh computers (since Apple offers only 90 days of phone support) and rear projection microdisplay TVs (which have a higher repair rate). However, extended warranties can offer peace of mind, such as not facing a huge financial loss and not having to search for a company to do repairs if a product breaks down. So, when you get a sales pitch, take your time. Check out your options. A retailer's warranty can offer needed support if you find yourself fighting back against a manufacturer.

PART 6

protecting your big-dollar purchases of cars and houses

MY PARENTS BOUGHT a house in a Montreal suburb for $19,000 in 1952. Today, you can spend that much or more on a new car of average quality.

In 1979, my husband and I bought a Toronto townhouse for $72,500. We bought a bigger house for $256,000 in 1986. An average property in Canada's largest city now sells for $516,000. And in our neighbourhood, it is hard to find a listing for less than $1 million.

When you pay so much to drive around and put a roof over your head, you might expect to be free from repair costs for a long time. A new car comes with a manufacturer's warranty. A new house also comes with a builder's warranty in many provinces.

But the protection is not foolproof. Buyers do not know with certainty that they are protected from manufacturing defects. Sometimes, they must hire a lawyer or go to small claims court to fight for the coverage that should come with their expensive purchase. Talk about an unequal fight. The customer, often unrepresented, is up against a big company with the budget to hire a team of skilled lawyers. The arguments are so technical that both sides need expert testimony to settle disputes.

Some frustrated buyers use social media to spread the word about their run-ins with stubborn companies. Ken Barber has a troublesome 2010 Ford Escape, which cost him $30,000 and required 14 service calls in a four-month period. He has a website, www.lemonfordescape.com, and a Twitter account, @fordescapelemon. But Ford Canada blocked his tweets after he turned down a small rebate to buy another car.

In this section, you will find out how to fight back when your new car does not work properly. Stephen Moody, general manager of the Canadian Motor Vehicle Arbitration Plan (CAMVAP), gives advice on how to get the best results at a hearing.

You will also hear from a well-known specialist in infectious diseases, Neil Rau, about the tricks he used to persuade a financing company to reduce an almost $4,000 bill for wear and tear on his 39-month lease for a MINI Cooper S car (then worth about $18,000). Media was also part of his game plan.

When it comes to real estate, you might buy a newly built house or condo that has defects that the builder will not fix. Karen Somerville, president of Canadians for Properly Built Homes, says that there is more protection for buying a toaster at a store than buying a house from a bad builder. She tells buyers not to move in quickly. Your leverage with the builder is much greater before you take legal possession of the home.

Mark Weisleder, a real estate lawyer and writer, tells you how to avoid making an offer well over the asking price for a house when you think that you are in a bidding war. He provides a clause that you can put into your offer, allowing you to cancel the deal or change the price if the seller cannot prove that there were other offers.

Electricity and natural gas can be a major expense for homeowners, especially if you do not understand how the utilities calculate costs. Paul Green, the ombudsman at Energy Gas Distribution in Toronto, advises you to read your utility bills and bill inserts (which are often thrown out unread). Learn how to escalate your complaints, following a defined set of steps to reach a higher level. And do not show your utility bills to a salesperson at your door, since they contain personal information.

Moving homes can go smoothly without any delay or damage to your stuff. But in some cases, a mover is careless and breaks things, forcing you to file an insurance claim. It's important to buy the right insurance, as Derek Dedman found when he hired the mover from hell. He got his money back after finding evidence of falsified documents. I'll provide tips on hiring a mover and increasing the odds of surviving a move with your sanity intact.

It is hard to buy cars and houses without getting burned on some aspect of the deal. You do not learn the tricks of the trade in school. Instead, you learn by trial and error. When you do these transactions only once in a while, you cannot build enough skills and experience to fight back successfully against the pros.

So, arm yourself with knowledge before venturing into the boxing ring. Good luck with your big-ticket purchases.

CHAPTER 70

How to Fight Back when Your Car Does Not Work Properly

By Stephen Moody

Stephen Moody is general manager of the Canadian Motor Vehicle Arbitration Plan (CAMVAP).

THE CANADIAN MOTOR Vehicle Arbitration Plan (CAMVAP) is a Canada-wide program that helps consumers resolve disputes with vehicle manufacturers about alleged manufacturing defects or how the manufacturer is implementing a new vehicle warranty.

If a consumer finds that the vehicle is not operating properly and has a current defect—a defect that exists now and continues to exist at the time of a CAMVAP hearing—or if there is a dispute with the manufacturer over implementing the new vehicle warranty, CAMVAP is available if the consumer's vehicle is from the current model year or the past four model years.

Most, but not all, vehicle manufacturers participate in the CAMVAP program. Based on the evidence presented at a hearing, a CAMVAP arbitrator can order:

1. Repairs to the consumer's vehicle.

2. Reimbursement for repairs that have already been done.

3. Reimbursement for out-of-pocket expenses, including diagnostic testing to try and resolve the issue with the vehicle.

4. Buyback of the consumer's vehicle, if it has been in service for less than three years and has travelled less than 60,000 kilometres.

5. The manufacturer has no liability with respect to the issues being arbitrated.

Manufacturers build vehicles that are designed to last and provide many kilometres of trouble-free use. To get that trouble-free use, it is the consumer's responsibility to ensure that ongoing scheduled vehicle maintenance is done, and on time.

A vehicle is a machine. Following the recommended maintenance schedule is the key to getting the expected performance from any vehicle. As consumers, we expect our vehicles to operate in all weather conditions, from scorching hot summer temperatures to freezing winter conditions. Care and routine maintenance are needed to create the optimum conditions for any vehicle to provide the service that we expect.

Here are some tips for operating a vehicle and deciding what to do if your vehicle issue is not resolved by the dealer and the manufacturer.

- **Follow the scheduled maintenance program set out by the manufacturer.** Ensure this maintenance is done on time and in accordance with the schedule set out in the owner's handbook.

- **When something seems wrong with the vehicle, get it checked.** Don't wait. Problems frequently become more severe if they are left unattended.

- **Set up a file for your vehicle.** Keep copies of the work orders for every time that your vehicle is repaired, whether it is done at a dealer or another repairer. Be certain that the work order details what was done to the vehicle.

- **Take and keep notes on your discussions with the dealer and the manufacturer.** Keep a record of what was said, when it was said, what the dealer and manufacturer did and what you did to try and resolve the issues with the vehicle.

- **Use Original Equipment Manufacturer (OEM) parts.** Use of non-OEM parts may, in some cases, result in denial of warranty coverage. Non-OEM parts are not covered for dispute resolution through CAMVAP.

Should a consumer find that issues with a vehicle have not been resolved at the dealer level and assistance from the manufacturer is needed to help in resolution of the issue, then, in addition to the steps above, the consumer should:

- **Read the owner's manual.** Follow the dispute resolution process set out by the manufacturer.

- **Contact the manufacturer's Customer Assistance or Care Centre.** This point is a key element in being eligible for CAMVAP.

- **Be reasonable.** Give the dealer the opportunity to resolve the problem. Both the dealer and the manufacturer want the vehicle to be properly repaired the first time it goes to the dealer, but sometimes it will take more than one visit to properly identify the repairs needed to correct the problems with the vehicle.

- **Contact CAMVAP.** You can call a toll-free number, 1-800-207-0685, or start the application process online at www.camvap.ca.

When getting ready for a CAMVAP hearing, the consumer should:

- **Read the CAMVAP program materials.** How to prepare and present a CAMVAP case is outlined in the program's guidebooks for consumers.

- **Know the possible outcomes that can be expected through CAMVAP arbitration.** This is important, particularly if you are asking for a buyback. It is recommended that you calculate the potential buyback amount early in the process to ensure that it is the right financial outcome in your circumstances. There are tools on the CAMVAP website to quickly and easily do this calculation. In many cases, reimbursement for repairs or the manufacturer being ordered to repair the vehicle may be better outcomes to resolve your issues.

- **Be prepared to present an organized case.** You must be prepared and able to explain to the arbitrator what is wrong with the vehicle. Exactly what is the current defect? Or what is the issue with the manufacturer's implementation of the new vehicle warranty? What steps have you taken to resolve these issues and what were the results achieved? The onus or burden of proof is on you to make the case.

- **Look at the case from the manufacturer's perspective.** Be prepared to respond and provide counterpoints to the evidence that you expect the manufacturer will present at the hearing.

- **Be prepared to bring credible witnesses to the hearing.** If the problem is intermittent or occurs when the vehicle is operated outside the posted speed limits, bring witnesses who have seen and experienced the issues that are to be arbitrated. Witnesses and photo or video evidence strengthens your case immeasurably.

- **Consider independent diagnostic testing as part of your planning.** CAMVAP arbitrators can order up to $500 in diagnostic fees as part of the remedies available through the program.

- **Be aware that how a vehicle has been used may be an issue at a CAMVAP hearing.** Severe off-road use or racing the vehicle will be raised as issues at a hearing if they are known. More than one case has been lost through social media postings!

CHAPTER 71

How to Fight Back Against Car Leasing Charges

By Neil Rau

Neil Rau is a physician who lives in Oakville, Ont., and is an expert in infectious diseases. He often appears on CTV News.

IN 2007, I LEASED a nice, peppy MINI Cooper S runabout that could ferry our children in and out of tight urban parking spaces. Our 2004 Saab 9-3 lease had just ended without incident.

But as the kids got older, the legroom in the back of the Cooper S was increasingly hard for my son and daughter to endure. Overnight road trips were a challenge, as we were limited to a single carry-on-sized suitcase.

Our 39-month lease on the Cooper S was beginning to feel like an eternity. So I went into the MINI Downtown dealership in Toronto in October 2010 to talk about leasing the new 2010 MINI Cooper S Clubman.

The service manager gave the car a good look and said that tire wear was a potential issue. A third party, DataScan Field Services, would make a final assessment of any outstanding wear and tear issues.

So I turned in my Cooper S on November 1, 2010, and left the dealership with a new Clubman.

Ten days later, MINI Financial Services sent me a letter, demanding $3,725 in wear and tear charges, keeping in mind that the car was now worth around $18,000. The $3,725 figure was derived from $1,800 in "hail damage" and $375 for each tire ("excessive tread wear") and a few dents and scratches. I was blindsided. It was time to fight back. Here is what I did:

call and try to negotiate.

The leasing company removed a $125 charge for scheduled maintenance that was performed the month before. (Someone had forgotten to reset the indicator.) They also cut the charge for one scratch by $175.

don't let a small concession suffice.

I was still left with a whopping bill. I told MINI Financial that it was bilking me.

explore third-party options.

I asked to keep the car at the dealer, since I had turned it in before the due date. I wanted to look at getting used tires to cut the cost. I also wanted to check out the validity of the $1,600 assessment for hail damage.

My insurer, after reviewing Weather Network data, said that there had been no hailstorms in five years in southern Ontario. But it denied responsibility for a car that I no longer possessed. I was stonewalled.

call the media if you are getting nowhere.

When I told MINI that I would ask a reporter to write a story, it was not fazed. An article appeared in the *Toronto Star* on December 10, 2010, by Ellen Roseman ("Tips on saving when returning a leased car," http://www.ellenroseman.com/?p=1108).

stand strong in the face of adversity.

The article did nothing to stop an endless barrage of automated telephone messages and letters from MINI Financial. I refused to pay. Six months later, the company's strategy changed a bit. I received a more personalized letter from an asset recovery specialist at BMW Financial Services (the parent company for MINI Financial Services), threatening legal action and referral to a collection agency.

stand strong and reiterate the options—a settlement or more bad press.

BMW Financial did not want to settle. So I suggested calling the *Toronto Star* to discuss the latest letter. When I told the woman on the phone to check out Ellen Roseman's column online, a long pause followed. She refused to speak to a reporter and asked if I was willing to pay at all.

give a bit, take a bit.

I wanted to find common ground, but I also said I would go to court and embarrass BMW Financial if necessary. A few lawyer friends had already offered to defend me in court *pro bono*. They liked the media coverage that this story had received.

The woman said she would speak to her manager and call me back. An hour later, she asked me what I thought was a reasonable sum. I said I had expected a $1,000 bill (tops) for the tire wear and minor scratches, while the $1,800 hail damage assessment and $375 per tire assessment were still preposterous.

emphasize your importance as a future customer.

I said I would readily pay $1,000. If BMW insisted, I would pay 50 per cent of the original bill, but with everlasting resentment. We settled on $2,000, slightly more than half of the original bill—and you won't see me leasing or buying another BMW product again.

I have to admit that my spouse was fed up with all the phone messages and letters. We were relieved to bring this to an end, given our busy careers and family life. And so, a settlement was made, followed by a release letter in the mail.

think twice about buying end-of-lease insurance.

Such a policy can help absolve you of some costs. However, hail damage is not covered. It's an illusion to think you will save money, since buying insurance increases the cost of the lease. Leasing companies should build that insurance into their processes. They should also be reasonable: How likely is it for a car to have minimal wear after three years of regular urban use?

check the leasing company's reputation online.

My neighbour, who uses MINIs to promote his company's brand, had similar issues at the end of multiple leases. He thinks the company loses money on artificially inflated residual values (designed to make leasing more appealing with lower monthly payments) and these lease-end tactics are a way to recover the loss. I think he's on to something. You can find other customers' comments on the Internet.

realize that not all leasing companies are the same.

My story has good news. When I recently came to the end of a Mercedes B Class lease, I received a clear letter in the mail informing me of my right to obtain a third-party inspection up to three months before lease end.

Once I had the lease inspection, I found it available online within 48 hours. And many of the issues that BMW Financial might have pursued were readily waived by Mercedes Financial as "expected wear and tear."

Would I lease again from Mercedes? You bet.

CHAPTER 72

How Not to Get Stung when Buying a Newly Built Home

By Dr. Karen Somerville, Canadians for Properly Built Homes

Dr. Karen Somerville is president of Canadians for Properly Built Homes (CPBH), a national, not-for-profit corporation dedicated to healthy, safe, durable and energy-efficient residential housing for Canadians. CPBH receives no government funding and relies on donations from consumers to cover its operating expenses. To send an e-mail, write to info@canadiansforproperlybuilthomes.com.

BUYING A HOME is the largest purchase most of us make. Many consumers have concluded that there is more protection for buying a toaster at a store than for buying a home. Here are ways to protect yourself from a bad builder.

stage 1—before deciding to purchase a newly built home.

- Select a builder. Look beyond a neighbourhood or home design and look at the builder's past performance. Unfortunately, there is no reliable or objective information about builder performance available to the public. You have to conduct your own research. For example, you can review media reports and talk to qualified new home inspectors.

- Determine what your municipality will inspect during construction.

- Understand the limitations of your home warranty (if you get one). Carefully review the fine print.

- Review your home insurance policy to see if there are any limitations related to newly built homes.

- Establish your purchase team: (1) A real estate lawyer experienced in new home construction, and (2) A qualified new home inspector who will note building code violations in your inspection report.

- Prepare the contract to purchase before signing. Review the document carefully with your lawyer. Decide whether you need additional clauses in the contract, such as permitting your own home inspector to inspect during construction and warranty extensions.

stage 2—before taking possession of your newly built home.

- Prepare for the Pre-Delivery Inspection (PDI).

  - Obtain copies of all municipal inspection reports for your home and review them carefully with your home inspector.

  - Obtain a copy of the final Occupancy Permit issued by your municipality.

  - Ensure that there is adequate time for you and your home inspector to carefully inspect the home during your PDI.

  - Schedule the PDI with your builder and home inspector at least a week before the date you plan to take possession of the home. This will give adequate time to reflect on the PDI inspection results.

- Carefully inspect the home and take detailed notes during the PDI.

- Ask the builder to address all construction defects and deficiencies before your possession date. Extend the possession date if necessary. Your leverage with the builder is much greater before you take legal possession of the home.

stage 3—resolving construction defects after taking possession.

- Monitor your home carefully. If there are construction defects, try to work with your builder.

- Beware of warranty time limits. If the construction defects are not properly addressed by your builder, prepare claims to your warranty provider and *submit them on time*.

- Submit claims to your municipality for building code violations.

- If there are problems with the builder and warranty provider, request assistance from your provincial or territorial elected representative. Consumer protection for housing in Canada is primarily the responsibility of the provinces and territories.

- If the problems remain unresolved, consider going to the media and reporting to the Better Business Bureau.

- As a last resort, explore legal options.

- Appeal your municipal property tax assessment, if appropriate.

CHAPTER 73

How to Fight Back in a Phony Real Estate Bidding War

By Mark Weisleder

Mark Weisleder is a real estate lawyer in Toronto and a regular contributor to The Star.com

I DEVELOPED A BIDDING war clause a few years ago that is widely used in real estate contracts. The clause says that the buyer is presenting his offer based on the assumption that multiple offers will be presented to the seller that same evening.

The clause goes on to say that if the seller receives no other offers by a certain time, say 10:00 p.m., the buyer can change his mind, cancel the deal or change the price.

If the seller accepts the buyer's offer, he must provide the buyer with proof that he has received another offer. This means providing, at minimum, the name, address and phone number of the real estate agent who presented the rival offer.

Here is my advice:

- Use a bidding war clause if you suspect that the seller really does not have another offer.

- By using this clause, you have assurance that if your offer is accepted, the seller will have to prove that he indeed did have at least one other offer available.

- This is the wording I like to use for the bidding war clause:

"This offer is being submitted on the basis that it is part of multiple offers. If the seller receives no other offer by 10:00 p.m., the seller will notify the buyer's agent and the buyer will have one hour to revise or revoke their offer. If the seller accepts the buyer's offer, the seller will provide the name, address and phone number of the agent and brokerage company that submitted the competing offer."

- In a case in Toronto, a couple paid $90,000 over the asking price of a house, believing that they were in a bidding war. They were shocked to find out that they were the only bidders. The seller was eventually persuaded to accept half of that—$45,000 over the asking price.

- By using a bidding war clause whenever you are suspicious about the possibility of a bidding war, you can successfully avoid this happening to you.

- Do not make a bid if the listing agent has his or her own offer, unless all offers are presented to the seller by the office manager.

- Do not participate in a faxed offer process. Always have your agent present your offer in person to the seller.

CHAPTER 74

How to Resolve Issues with Your Energy Utility

By Paul Green

Paul Green is the ombudsman at Enbridge Gas Distribution, the largest natural gas utility in Canada, which delivers to more than 1.9 million customers.

AT ENBRIDGE, our goal is to provide courteous, quality service in each customer interaction. Unfortunately, there are times when we fall short. In my role as ombudsman, I try to help our customers understand how to get help when we do not meet our commitments. Here are some ideas that you can use with your own gas or electrical utility:

- **Share your opinions and feedback.** Most utilities value their customers' opinions. At Enbridge, we use input from calls, e-mails and personal interactions, as well as research, to help ensure that we are delivering what our customers expect from us. In fact, that's how the Office of the Ombudsman was created. Customers were telling us loud and clear that we needed to improve our escalation process and we did. An escalation process allows a customer to speak to a supervisor after a call centre representative is unable to help. The third step at Enbridge is to contact our customer ombudsman.

- **Read your bill regularly.** It is important to check your utility bills, even if you have payments automatically withdrawn from your bank account or you have charges spread out all year to make budgeting easier. Many websites, including Enbridge Gas Distribution's, have information to help you understand the different charges on your bill. You can take advantage of features, such as charts or tables, offered by your utility company to compare your use year over year.

- **Be an informed customer.** Read the material provided with your bills and visit your service providers' websites. This can help you and your family use energy more efficiently and safely. At Enbridge, our *Pipeline* newsletter (included in the monthly bill envelope) has useful tips about energy and safety. Our website also describes the escalation process to help customers get to the right person to resolve their inquiries.

- **If something doesn't seem right, contact your utility.** If you notice a higher or lower than normal amount or an unexpected charge on your bill, contact the customer service representatives at your utility to ask about it. The vast majority of issues can be fixed quickly and easily the first time you contact your utility. Find out when and how you will know if the issue has been resolved or if you need to take any additional steps. Make a quick note of the expected outcomes and watch to make sure they happen.

- **Escalate your concern.** A more complicated issue or an unsatisfactory experience may require more follow up. Speaking with a supervisor or manager is usually the next step. Utilities all have their own processes for handling escalated issues. Ask a customer service representative or look online to determine the utility's escalation processes. Enbridge Gas customers who cannot resolve their issue with a service representative or supervisor can contact the Ombudsman's Office. Each inquiry is assigned to an Ombudsman's Office representative who resolves the issue and keeps the customer informed of the progress.

- **Be very cautious when people come door-to-door.** If you open your door and are greeted by a salesperson, ask what company they represent, ask for photo identification and keep a copy of any material they show you. Don't feel pressured to sign anything and don't show your utility bills, since they contain personal information. Ask them to leave a pamphlet or application form, so that you can review them on your own time and make an informed decision.

- **Read the contract.** If you choose to purchase something being sold door-to-door, make sure that you are given a copy of the contract. Take time to read the fine print and understand what you are agreeing to before signing. Despite the impression you may be given by the sellers, you do not have to buy products and services sold at your door. Enbridge does not conduct door-to-door sales.

CHAPTER 75

How to Fight Back Against Rogue Movers

MOVING IS STRESSFUL. You hand over your possessions, hoping that they will be handled with care and escorted safely to your new home. Finding a few cracks and scratches is unfortunate, but not unforgivable, if you are properly insured.

Problems can arise, however, when you skimp too much on costs. Moving comes at a time when you are already feeling overstretched. After talking to a few firms, you may decide to use one that undercuts the others by a wide margin. This can backfire in a big way if you end up with a rogue mover.

These unethical firms quote you a great price for moving your stuff, but the price doubles once they show up at the destination. They can hold your goods hostage in a storage locker and not release them unless you pay up. Or they can force you to unload your belongings from the truck and find another mover on short notice.

Here are ways to avoid getting ripped off by unscrupulous movers:

- Seek recommendations from friends and family members.

- Ask for client references. Look for reviews and testimonials online.

- Ask for estimates from at least three reliable movers in your area.

- Find out if the company belongs to a well-known trade group, such as the Canadian Association of Movers, www.mover.net.

- Do not get an estimate over the phone. Make sure they come to your home and survey your stuff.

- Do not sign a blank form. Get everything down in writing.

Derek Dedman was living in Regina, Sask., when he was offered a job in Ottawa. He and his wife decided to make the move a month after their second baby was due. Since they had no friends or family with any recent moving experience, they went to the Internet and got three initial quotes from different movers. All quoted similar shipment weights, based on their home size.

"The company I chose offered a small discount for early bookings," he said. "Price was the ultimate factor in making my decision. Big mistake."

At the company's website, there was an even ratio of positive to negative reviews. This was the first red flag. Dedman was impressed by the fact that the firm had been operating for more than a decade. Also, the sales manager was courteous and seemed to care.

No one came to his home to provide an estimate (the second red flag). He filled out a spreadsheet listing all his possessions and was given a quote for the move at just under $5,000. He agreed to proceed.

Things went downhill quickly. The movers arrived late, only two days before they had to be out of their house, and said that they would not have enough room in their truck for all the possessions. They loaded what they could, leaving the customers scrambling to get the house ready for the new owners—all in one day.

Dedman began his drive to Ottawa. The night before he arrived, he got a call from the movers. They said that his stuff would be delivered the next morning, as long as he paid right away. The cost was now more than $9,500, not including the goods that were still in Saskatchewan. This was double what he had been quoted.

The actual charges were based on actual weights, the company said, and he had to pay if he wanted the goods delivered. So, he paid.

"It appeared they hadn't carefully shipped our stuff. We estimated the damage to be close to $10,000. I could have opted for extra insurance, but I didn't," Dedman said. That was another mistake.

After threatening to go to the Better Business Bureau, he received a refund offer of $750. The offer grew to $1,000. Still, he decided to fight and found two pieces of regulation that proved to be helpful.

According to the Ontario Highway Traffic Act, it is the responsibility of the originating carrier to show the correct net weights by using a certified public scale and attaching the weigh scale ticket to the carrier's copy of the contract. And according to Ontario's consumer protection act, a moving company cannot charge more than 10 per cent above the written estimate.

Dedman had not been provided with the certified weigh scale tickets. His request was always brushed off or ignored. He contacted the mover to say it had a legal obligation to provide certified scale receipts. After days of phone calls and threats, he received a rough Microsoft Word document with minimal information. No address, no signatures and nothing else.

The only identifying mark was from a CAT scale in Regina. He found that there was only one CAT (Certified Automated Truck) scale in Regina and called the number. He talked to an employee who was sympathetic and faxed him a copy of a CAT scale ticket for comparison.

Then, he had a revelation. The "ticket" that the mover provided showed that the truck was supposedly weighed with his possessions over a half hour *before* it left his house.

He called the manager at the moving company to say that he had proof the tickets were fake. He gave the company a choice: refund the difference between the quote and actual charge, or face the prospect of being taken to court and reported to the RCMP.

Eventually, the manager chose the first option. Dedman received a refund cheque in the amount of $4,907.84.

"I didn't receive a refund for the $40 scale fee. They can keep it," he said.

Here are more tips on how to protect yourself:

- Consult the Better Business Bureau for any complaints against companies you may be considering.

- Avoid movers that want to deal in cash only or offer to avoid the Goods and Services Tax (GST) or Harmonized Sales Tax (HST).

- Read the fine print of any contract before you sign. Ensure you understand the terms and conditions.

- Investigate the insurance offered as part of the contract. Carriers are required to have a minimum amount, which covers your goods at a rate of $0.60 per pound. This translates into about $30 for a typical television set.

- Most carriers will offer some sort of additional insurance. The cost is likely worth it.

- Make sure you get replacement value protection and not just depreciated value.

- Ask if the company has its own equipment. Will it subcontract to another company? If so, find out the name and ask for references.

- It is a good idea to visit and check out the company's offices, storage facilities and vehicles before you move.

- Read *The Consumer Checklist for Choosing a Moving Company*, and the associated *Good Practice Guidelines for Canadian Movers,* prepared by a group of stakeholders led by the Office of Consumer Affairs at Industry Canada, www.ic.gc.ca.

- On moving day, have everything ready to go when the movers arrive. You will be charged an hourly rate for the time that the movers wait.

- Report damage quickly. Normally, claims must be made within 30 days for a local move and 60 days for a long-distance move.

- Do a walk-through of your premises when the loading has been completed. Ensure that everything has been loaded and nothing is left in closets, behind doors, in attics or garages.

- Take all of your valuables with you (such as jewellery, artwork, prescription drugs and important papers).

- Back up your computer data and take the computer and the data with you.

- When the unloading has been completed, do a walk-through of your premises, all hallways and pathways into your premises and the moving vehicle, as well, to ensure that everything is unloaded.

- Enjoy your new home.

PART 7

using your communication skills and the courts

CUSTOMERS OFTEN get nowhere with companies, even when they have a good case, because they are poor communicators. They call when they should write. They fail to organize and present their cases properly. They cannot control their emotions. They "lose it" on the phone or in face-to-face confrontations.

When you vent your frustration on low-level staff and use them as punching bags, you slash your chances of success. Most companies will not take you seriously when you start yelling, swearing and insulting the staff. This is not the way to make friends and influence people.

One day, I got a call from a customer of a large home service company (Direct Energy) whose furnace had broken down on a cold winter day. Her husband had spent hours on the phone, but did not seem to be making progress. Finally, he erupted. He said he would visit the office with a gun to show that he meant business.

Making a death threat is the worst possible tactic you can use in try-ing to get what you want. Companies never react positively to violence. Though the wife argued that the threat was metaphorical, not literal, she could not turn things around. Direct Energy closed the account, forcing the couple to seek furnace repairs elsewhere.

In this section, U.S. consumer advocate Christopher Elliott will tell you how to write effective letters. He does not want you to waste your time in "call centre hell," dealing with the "I can't help desk." He wants you to complain in writing to management. Manners matter, in his opinion. And if you do not tell the company what you want, you will not get it.

Franke James is a dogged complainer. I helped her win an out-of-court settlement with a furnace company that damaged her home but she did most of the work, writing letters to everyone that counted and creating a circle of eyes on the company. She tells you how to fight back in the court of public opinion.

Ted Whipp, a newspaper reporter, saves every piece of paper that he ever needs to provide proof of purchase. This ability to be organized and prepared helps him win battles with companies long after the fact. He was able to get free repairs on an eight-year-old dishwasher and free replacement of 13-year-old windows, simply by being persistent. You can get better service just by asking, he says.

Scott Smith was on a business trip when United Airlines lost his luggage. Still waiting for it two weeks later, he used Twitter to spread the news. When he used my name in his tweets, I re-tweeted them to others. The Twitter campaign worked, since the airline delivered his bags less than 12 hours later. Smith, known on Twitter as @scottaesmith, gives tips on how to make large companies twig to your tweets.

Orie Niedzviecki is a lawyer who likes to fight on behalf of consumers. He has seen many consumers approach lawyers in the wrong way, alleging corporate conspiracies or relying on gut feelings to support their accusations. He suggests hiring a licensed paralegal to represent you in a small claims court case, because lawyer's fees will be too high and any legal costs awarded to you will be relatively small.

Jeremy Cooperstock, a McGill University engineering professor, was upset when United Airlines damaged his baggage and ignored him for 14 months. He started the popular Untied.com website. He likes to use legal muscle against companies that get in his way. Targets of his successful challenges include Via Rail, Budget and Discount car rentals, TD Canada Trust, FedEx, UPS, Apple, Bell and Multicities Movers.

"Sadly, I have learned that it is the exception, rather than the rule, in which a serious complaint is resolved prior to legal action," Cooperstock says.

After you make an unsuccessful effort at diplomatic resolution, proceed directly to minimal effort, minimal cost legal action, he advises. This typically means filing a small claims court action.

"Such cases are invariably settled before the court date, especially when the damages claimed are modest," he says. "Simply threatening to sue is usually pointless, although I've had some successes with registered letters that give notice of impending legal action."

The advice offered will help you make inroads with companies that may have ignored you in the past. You will learn to be more patient, persistent, prepared—and yes, polite—in your life as a consumer. These qualities will serve you better than giving in to emotion and gut instinct.

By now, I hope that you are ready to fight back and protect yourself against corporate tricks. You have mastered the art of complaining. Now you have to go out and use it.

Just remember a message that runs throughout this book. Few companies reward your loyalty. Many exploit your loyalty and treat you poorly. They let you pay more and get fewer services than newer customers, who demand the best in order to switch.

Your leverage depends on getting companies to recognize your loyalty. They have to realize that it costs more to replace you than to give you a few discounts or concessions. They can rely on you to stick around, unlike the butterfly customers who flit from one supplier to the next, looking for the sweetest deals.

But if you are ignored, you have to leave and find a new supplier. Switching can be difficult, but this fight-or-flight strategy guarantees that you will get great offers afterward. Bell Canada is known for wooing former customers with unbelievable bargains.

Good luck with your efforts to fight back. Stay calm, cool and collected. Use your communication skills—and legal help when required—to get what you want from the companies lucky enough to win your business.

CHAPTER 76

How to Write the Perfect Complaint Letter

By Christopher Elliott

Christopher Elliott is a U.S. consumer advocate and journalist. He's the author of Scammed: How to Save Your Money and Find Better Service in a World of Schemes, Swindles and Shady Deals *(Wiley, 2011). This list of tips was adapted with permission from his book.*

I HAVE A LIFETIME of experience being on hold with companies, as do the people I try to assist in my consumer advocacy work. We are outraged by the long wait times and we believe that companies force us into the waiting game to get rid of us. And we are right.

When you want an answer, you might want to use e-mail or even a conventional letter. Here are tips on writing the perfect letter:

- **Keep meticulous records.** Retain all receipts, signed contracts, ticket stubs and any other evidence of your purchase.

- **Enclose evidence.** Take a few digital snapshots of your new washing machine that exploded in your house. And if you see an online price that seems too good to be true, take a screenshot. Attach them to your e-mail, since they are irrefutable evidence of a purchase or product defect.

- **Do solid-as-a-rock research.** You'd be amazed what you can find with a quick Internet search: everything from successful letters to the form replies they generated to tips for writing a letter. I started a wiki, www.onyoursi.de/wiki, with reader tips on sharing advice for successful grievance results.

- **Keep it tight.** The most effective e-mails and letters are unbelievably short—no more than three paragraphs or 175 words. Remember, that's a real person on the other end trying to get to the point, so if you write something that goes on forever, it's possible they won't make it all the way to the end.

- **Be as polite as possible.** Manners *really* matter. Customer service agents tell me that cordial and grammatically correct missives catch their attention and make them want to offer better service.

- **Avoid anger.** Letters that are packed with four-letter words, threats and ALL UPPER CASE receive the bare minimum in the way of response— or nothing at all. (Don't use curse words. It's f***ing unnecessary. We all get upset. Be measured.)

- **Cite rules of the road.** Your complaint has the best chance of getting a fair shake if you can convince the company that it didn't follow its own rules or that it somehow broke the law. Sometimes, the rules are less than obvious. If you have questions, ask the company for a copy of the contract or look on its site.

- **Tell them what you want.** Leaving out this detail can doom your request to failure. It leaves the question of "How do you fix this?" up to the customer service representative—and rest assured, their answer will disappoint you more often than not.

- **Copy everyone.** Yes, customer service representatives review the list of everyone you've copied on an e-mail or letter. When they see you've shared a grievance with a few other folks, it will give the complaint more weight. Just think of it as the exclamation mark at the end of your letter.

- **Do your best to succeed.** A concise, polite, well-researched and-targeted e-mail that specifically says how a company can address your grievance has the best chance of success. A rambling, vague and overly emotional one is likely to never get answered, and in your heart you know nobody will read it.

CHAPTER 77

How to Create a Circle of Eyes on a Company You Want to Fight

By Franke James

Franke James is an artist and author of **Bothered by My Green Conscience: How an SUV-driving, Imported-Strawberry-Eating Urban Dweller Can Go Green** *(New Society Publishers, 2009). Her website is www.frankejames.com.*

I WAS FIGHTING A COMPANY over the faulty installation of a gas furnace and ductwork, which had caused major structural damage to our home. I wanted it to pay for repairs. The company had deep pockets and no fear of going to court. Its lawyer said in a surly e-mail, "Go ahead. Sue us."

Going to court could have amounted to financial suicide for our family or, at the very least, hardship. There was no way I wanted to fight this battle in court or even in an arbitration hearing.

I wanted to fight it where the odds were more in my favour: the court of public opinion. And for most people, that's a good strategy. It's a lot cheaper than hiring lawyers, but it does depend on having good communication skills.

In my experience, most companies will do the right thing—but only under threat of having their behavior (which often amounts to bullying) exposed to the world. Everyone—from private enterprises to public companies, to local and federal governments—is sensitive to public opinion.

So, here are my tips:

1. get as many eyes looking at your problem as possible.

In the case of the furnace company, I drew a circle of the multiple "eyes" that I wanted to be aware of the problem. That circle included: my local city councillor, the city building department, the safety licensing agency for gas furnaces, the Better Business Bureau, the furnace company's CEO and consumer advocate columnist and author Ellen Roseman, whose reach focuses many eyes on any problem. Create a circle of eyes for the problem you're trying to solve.

2. prepare an information package.

I sent an initial information package about the problem to each of those "eyes." That package included a letter, before and after photos, e-mails between the company and me, and a timeline with significant dates and phone calls.

3. raise the stakes. keep the heat on.

As the situation evolved, I kept all of the "eyes" updated by e-mail. When the company lawyer wrote to me privately, I replied and cc'ed all of them, including the CEO. I wanted everyone to be aware and watching how the company was handling the problem. This tactic ensured that the CEO, governing bodies and the media were all watching how the lawyer handled the problem. This small consumer problem, which she had wanted to fight quietly in court before a single judge, was now being fought publicly in front of many judges.

4. use blogs and social media.

With the furnace company, I limited the circle of eyes to the six listed above. However, in dealing with other problems, I've increased the number of eyes dramatically by using the power of social media, blogs, radio, online news sites and online petitions. This helps spread the word and build support.

One example of the success of this online strategy is a victory in my own front yard. I wanted to persuade my municipal government to overturn an official's decision, which prevented us from replacing an interlocking brick driveway with a permeable driveway. The official said "it would be illegal" due to existing bylaws.

I wrote blog posts and used social media to raise awareness of the outdated bylaw, but the media buzz wasn't enough on its own. The pivotal moment came when I picked up the phone and called the mayor's office, telling them why we wanted to build a permeable, green driveway. They agreed it was a good idea and we won approval to build it as a pilot project.

5. hire an objective expert.

The faulty installation of our furnace and ductwork caused structural damage to our house. I called in a structural engineering firm to do an assessment and report. Their third-party evidence helped strengthen my case. And, of course, all of the "eyes" got copies of the report.

I have used experts to write reports to help resolve other problems over the years. A neighbouring apartment building was forced to repair its leaky eavestroughs after an engineer's report showed the water damage it was causing to our property.

6. pick other people's brains.

Ultimately, the resolution for the faulty furnace installation came from picking someone's brain. I was making good headway using the "eye" strategy, but I still didn't have what I wanted: a big cheque to pay for repairs.

So I asked for advice. My city councillor agreed to set up a meeting for me with the head of the building department. I brought in all my records, laid them out and asked his advice. He took one look at my file and told me I had made a mistake on the date of the building permit. My jaw dropped open.

He went over to his filing cabinet and produced the building permit record, which showed that our furnace had been installed in the fall. I was flabbergasted. I told him that was absolutely impossible, because the furnace was installed in the spring.

In fact, we were both right. The furnace installation company had applied for the permit six months after the job was done, a practice that is illegal since it prevents the building inspectors from assessing the safety of an installation.

The company quickly settled out of court, knowing that many eyes were watching what it was doing.

CHAPTER 78

How to Be Patient, Persistent and Prepared

By Ted Whipp

Ted Whipp is a reporter with the **Windsor Star** *who has a keen interest in consumer issues and likes to advocate on his own behalf.*

AN EIGHT-YEAR-OLD dishwasher leaked. The manufacturer still replaced it. No charge.

Thirteen-year-old windows developed condensation. The supplier not only replaced the three windows affected, but four others. All for free.

A drugstore chain awarded thousands of bonus points, despite a purchase the day before the reward offer was actually available.

No miracles, no ranting, no foot stomping, no grueling waits over the phone. But the resolutions in all three cases each required the same elements: patience, persistence and paperwork.

Here are my tips on getting what you want:

provide evidence.

The dishwasher manufacturer simply wanted proof when a service technician diagnosed a design defect. It helped that the warranty card that came with the then-new, original machine had been filled out. Also, an account was set up for service and a record of the purchase. The technician supplied the required paperwork, the manufacturer verified the original purchase and a comparable new model was delivered and installed.

The window manufacturer already had the extensive paperwork on file from the installation years ago. The windows did have a lifetime guarantee that covered the problem, a faulty seal during manufacture. All that was required was the patience to wait for the ideal weather for installation. Oh, and the four other windows beside the three with condensation had to be replaced, because they would not be compatible with the materials required for the new windows.

The drugstore chain could determine from my request that I was already quite loyal to its reward program. So the points were granted, but only after a long wait. Still, the paperwork was all there: a receipt record of the transaction moments before midnight and the next day's promotion.

persistence pays off.

Who would have even bothered with any of these requests, especially following up with an appliance manufacturer years later? And what could I expect beyond a meagre voucher for credit toward a new purchase?

Persistence paid off. But, really, what was there to lose beyond a few minutes on a toll-free phone call? Ditto for the windows and the drugstore chain.

paperwork is important.

Having the paperwork counts. And it has helped me so many times. Save receipts. Staple them to the instruction booklets for new appliances or similar big-ticket purchases and file them away. Keep them with income tax, insurance and other financial information in a safe, easily remembered location.

A recent receipt from a big-box discount chain showed a large supply of one item was charged twice. The store offered a refund the next day, agreeing that buying two of such a large size was unlikely. The same clerk was available to verify the mistake. Still, the supervisor appreciated the situation.

do not get emotional.

You soon learn not to get emotional, because negative emotions distract from the problem at hand. Calm patience pays off with customer service representatives, who seem to appreciate that you're one of the few customers on their shift (if not the only one) who isn't yelling and blaming them for all manner of crimes and injustices, real or imagined. Trust me on this.

And one more tip when making those long-distance calls to customer service: keep a pad and pen handy to take down any notes, addresses and information, such as the name of the representative and the call's incident or inquiry number—handy information for any follow-up call or future reference.

preparation helps in all kinds of situations.

If you have a special request—say for dinner, an allergy, the need for a kid's chair, whatever—ask ahead. If you want a hotel room close to the pool, ask ahead. Heck, let the hotel know that you'd appreciate an upgrade at no charge if it's available. Who knows? What's the harm in asking?

So, ask the airline for a seat upgrade. And ask the rental car agency rep if they may have a convertible available for a loyal customer.

Sure, there's every reason not to bother. But that's the thing about patience, persistence, preparation and paperwork. You never do know until you ask. Patiently, of course.

The bottom line: be patient, describe the problem and seek a reasonable resolution. Be persistent to look for some way, some answer, and provide the paperwork.

Most of all, be prepared. Save the receipts. Stay calm and focused on the problem and resolution.

CHAPTER 79

How to Use Twitter to Put Pressure on a Business

By Scott A.E. Smith

Scott A.E. Smith is a business student and worked as a travel analyst in the global business travel department of American Express Canada.

IF YOU HAVE EVER called your cable/Internet provider, your phone company or any other business with a 1-888 or 1-800 number, you probably know how frustrating it can be at times to get their attention. Fortunately, in this glorious new age of social media, there is a better way. It's called Twitter. Thanks to the popular micro-blogging service, good customer service is now easier to find than ever. My experience with it has been so overwhelmingly positive that I now tell friends that it's the only way to get things done.

When I recently had a less-than-satisfying Twitter experience with an airline, it came as something of a shock. Indeed, bad customer service on Twitter is the exception—not the rule. I would argue that the opposite is true when using traditional channels.

Here are my tips for how to use Twitter effectively to put pressure on a company to do right by you:

have a presence.

This is perhaps more important than anything else. It's unlikely that a company will feel compelled to act on your concern if you have only a handful of tweets and a small group of followers. So have a presence and manage it (almost like a business would) and build influence by gaining followers over time.

An active, well-subscribed Twitter account is extremely valuable if you want to get a company's attention. Think about it: if a celebrity with millions of followers tweets that he or she is unsatisfied with a flight, you can bet that the airline is going to take notice. Even if you're not a celebrity, you can still wield considerable influence in your own little corner of the Internet.

be nice.

You're not going to help yourself by unleashing an expletive-laden rant about the service you received from whatever company you're trying to put pressure on. If you can manage it, be funny.

Sarcasm, if employed correctly, can get a lot of retweets, favourites and replies on Twitter. And just like any conversation in real life, volume won't get you anywhere. Don't direct a barrage of tweets at the company's Twitter account. That will only get you blocked. One or two tweets will do. All of them are read, at the very least, so make them count by using humour and gravitas to get people on your side and by not being so disagreeable as to turn the company against you.

be patient and persistent.

It took no fewer than two weeks (of my two-week business trip to Phoenix) for my luggage to be located after United Airlines lost it. I'm convinced that the airline's efforts to find it were ramped up after I tweeted at Ellen Roseman of the *Toronto Star* and Christopher Elliott of *National Geographic* to say I felt like I was being ignored.

It would be quite a coincidence if their tweets and retweets in support of my case didn't at least partially explain how, after 14 days of waiting, my luggage was miraculously at my hotel less than 12 hours later.

It took significantly longer to be reimbursed for my expenses . . . six months, if you can believe it! But through patience and persistence, and the occasional Twitter update on my case as it got more and more preposterous, I finally got my cheque and a $300 travel credit for all my trouble.

CHAPTER 80

How to Deal with a Lawyer if You Have a Consumer Problem

By Orie H. Niedzviecki

Orie H. Niedzviecki is a partner at Ellyn Law LLP in Toronto. He practises in the areas of business litigation and employment law, but likes to take on consumer cases when they arise.

MANY PEOPLE HESITATE to call a lawyer when they have a consumer problem, assuming that it will be too expensive to pursue legal action through the courts. But there are cases when calling a lawyer might be your best remedy.

Here are some tips on dealing with lawyers:

- Always ask a lawyer if you have a claim worth pursuing. If you wait, you may be too late to initiate a lawsuit because of provincial statutes of limitation.

- Don't be embarrassed or think you are bothering a lawyer. Most lawyers are happy to speak to you for a few minutes to see if you might have a claim they are interested in.

- If a lawyer is not interested, do not spend any time arguing. Just find another lawyer. No lawyer is obligated to represent you. And if someone doesn't want to take your case, for whatever reason, then you probably don't want him or her as your lawyer.

- Be careful about alleging conspiracies between banks, the government and/or large corporations. Raising such complaints, without any evidence, will tag you as a problem client to many lawyers and they will not want to represent you.

- Don't bring multiple complaints to a lawyer all at once. They may see that as an indicator that you are someone who is too litigious. As a result, they will not want to represent you.

- Don't expect lawyers to be interested in your case if you have already retained a few lawyers on your case in the past.

- When a lawyer asks you to identify yourself, you should provide your name, address, phone number and e-mail address, even if you have not reached the stage where you are retaining the lawyer. Many lawyers require this information for their records. Some will even send a letter confirming that you are *not* retaining them if things don't work out.

- If you refuse to identify yourself, that is a big warning sign for most lawyers. If you contact a lawyer on behalf of someone else, be prepared to say who you are calling for and why that person can't call. Remember, all your communication with lawyers is strictly confidential even if you don't retain them.

- When you first speak to a lawyer, try to give a concise summary of the issue. Lawyers want a quick understanding of what is at stake to see if it is something they can help you with or not. They don't want to hear a one-hour recitation of everything that happened or how upset you are. If you retain the lawyer, there will be time for that later.

- It is difficult to recover damages for mental distress in a commercial dispute. If you want to make it an issue, you will need medical records showing you sought treatment from a doctor—and even that might not be enough. Mental distress is not a strong enough claim to bother with in commercial disputes. The effort to advance it isn't worth the return.

- If you make allegations against someone, find coherent reasons to explain why you are accusing them. Let the lawyer determine whether or not your reasons are legally sufficient. Do not rely on your gut feelings or a dream (as one client of mine did). This type of intuition is not admissible in court.

- If you are the one getting sued, don't delay. Find a lawyer immediately. These things won't just go away. And if you wait, you may harm your legal position significantly.

- Don't be intimidated if you are sued by a large company. There are many small legal firms that have lawyers just as qualified, or even more qualified, than those in big firms. The courts will not favour a large company. The judges try to treat everyone equally.

- Find a lawyer you like, someone who is recommended to you or who has some experience in the relevant area of law.

- Try to prepare a one-to-two-page summary of what happened. Stick to just the most important facts. That will be very useful to any lawyer you consult.

- Small claims court is cheaper and quicker than regular court, but the claim size is limited. You may want to reduce the amount you are suing for in order to get heard in small claims court. The limit is $35,000 in the Northwest Territories; $25,000 in Alberta, Nova Scotia, British Columbia, Newfoundland, Ontario and the Yukon; $20,000 in Saskatchewan and Nunavut; $10,000 in Manitoba; $8,000 in PEI; $7,000 in Quebec and $6,000 in New Brunswick.

- Licensed paralegals can represent you in small claims court. If your claim is on the small side, it may not be cost-effective to hire a lawyer, as the fees will be too high and any legal costs awarded to you will be relatively small. The cost of hiring a paralegal is much less than hiring a lawyer.

CHAPTER 81

How to Fight Back in Small Claims Court

HARRY ZBOROWSKI GOT A CALL from someone posing as his grand-daughter, saying that she had been in a car accident in Montreal. He agreed to send her $4,200 right away and became suspicious only a day later, when his granddaughter called to ask for more money to hire a lawyer. Her father was a lawyer and could have helped her.

This is known as the grandparent or emergency scam, which preys on a natural desire to help a friend or relative in a jam. You can protect yourself from fraud by making a quick call to the supposed victim, asking for confirmation of the story. But many people are so worried about their loved ones that they rush to Western Union to wire money, as instructed, without taking time to double check.

Zborowski's daughter, Sylvia Kestenberg, felt that Western Union did not safeguard her elderly father from swindlers and sued the company in small claims court. The judge ordered Western Union to pay $4,380 (including $180 for the money transfer fee), plus $5,000 in legal costs.

Consumers can go to small claims court on their own without a lawyer. However, they may be facing a company lawyer (or team of lawyers) on the other side. Judges may have little sympathy for consumers who are ignorant of the law and come to court without doing their homework.

Things were different in the Zborowski case. His family hired a lawyer and spent $12,000 in legal fees. (The $5,000 awarded by the judge covered less than half of their costs.) Western Union had no lawyer and sent the director of compliance, who admitted liability for the agent's poor training and lack of warnings at the agent's location.

Western Union has instituted more safeguards now. But the judge said it knew of the grandparent scam for years and failed to alert Zborowski, who had told the agent that he was wiring money to his granddaughter. "I find that giving absolutely no warning in the circumstances where 150 to 200 such frauds are perpetrated per month is below the standard required," the judge said.

Kestenberg pursued the case because others in her father's position did not have the ability to do so. In fact, her father probably would have walked away if his family had not supported him. She wanted to make a difference for other people who had suffered the same kind of harm.

This is an inspirational story about small claims court. But I also hear from people whose hopes are dashed. Mike Marsh wanted to get Ford to fix his one-year-old F150 truck, which shuddered and misfired when going up a hill or driving into a strong wind. His small claims court case was dismissed because he didn't provide any expert testimony to show that his truck vibrated in an abnormal manner.

"I shouldn't be surprised," said Marsh. "Me against two lawyers was a losing battle from the get-go. I didn't expect to have to prove that a vibration, which wasn't there at the time of purchase, was a defect. I expected that to be a given. The judge believed the statements by Ford and the dealership that the issue was minimal, if it existed at all."

Linda Miller had a similar problem with proof when pursuing a case in small claims court. She replaced her roof shingles after nine years because of attic leaks and mould, even though they were guaranteed for 25 years. The judge said that she had to prove that the shingles were defective and she had to bring witnesses.

"My only witness would be the roofer who replaced my roof and insulation, but he hasn't returned my calls. The original roofer has changed its name and the judge said I've probably taken the wrong company to court," she said. "The shingle company has class action suits against it for the same shingles that were on my house, but the judge said that didn't matter. There's no justice for the consumer."

Phil Edmonston, author of the Lemon-Aid new and used car guides, has 40 years of experience helping readers succeed with their complaints. He believes in going to small claims court, but only if you are prepared.

Always get an independent inspection to verify the defects that you claim to exist. Show the inspection to the manufacturer or retailer, asking for reconsideration. Then, if you are refused, you can go to small claims court with the proof that will be demanded of you.

Most provinces offer information on small claims court in brochures or on their websites, since they know that many people go without any legal representation. Read the rules and think about these questions before proceeding with your case.

- Do you know the legal name of the business and a current business address? You may not be able to serve a claim or enforce a judgment without the correct information about the company that you are suing.

- If you win, will you be able to collect from the business? Getting a judgment in your favour is only the first step, since you may have to try to collect the money by yourself (and at your own expense). There's no point going ahead if the company has no money, assets or income that can be garnished.

- Does the business owe money to others? There could be others waiting in line to collect their judgments. Try to find out by contacting a credit bureau, land registry office or court.

- Where should you file your claim? You must go to the small claims court office where the problem occurred or where the defendant carries on business. It may be too far away from your home to make it worthwhile to pursue the case.

- Do you have enough evidence to support your claim? "If you do not have supporting documents or witnesses, your claim may still be successful," says an Ontario guide to small claims court. "However, if it is just your word against the other person's, it may be more difficult to prove your case."

- When should you sue? How long ago did the dispute take place? There may be a time limit on how long you can wait before making a claim, which is set out in the provincial limitations act. Consult a lawyer if you are uncertain about the limitation period that applies to your case.

- Can you take time off to go to the court office to file documents or attend a trial? If you have an inflexible work schedule, you may not be able to pursue your day in court. You have to wait for your case to come up for trial and, if you cannot go, you have to wait for another court date. Failing to show up at the last minute can result in having to pay a penalty.

Despite all the hassles of going to court, you can come out with a great sense of vindication if you win. It is worth making the effort and publicizing your victory for two reasons. You can give others the encouragement to launch their own cases. And you can keep companies on their toes.

Ian Davidson sued a fitness chain after a thief broke into his locker and stole his credit card, cash and a Rolex watch. He was annoyed because the company had a policy that it was not responsible and members could make a claim on their home insurance policies.

He felt that the fitness chain had some responsibility. His locker theft was the tenth in two weeks for that location. Moreover, it happened at midday when the club was busy. In small claims court, he won a settlement that included one year's free membership, a letter of apology and a $2,000 donation to charity.

"There are now video cameras on the door in question," he said, referring to an emergency exit that was not secured.

Stefan Marilovic won $2,000 in damages for mental distress from Home Depot and Trane Canada after he bought a central air conditioning system that was not installed properly and was wrong for his house. He never paid for the cooling system and eventually had it removed.

"We've gone past the stage now where air conditioning is regarded as a luxury," the small claims court judge said, expressing sympathy for the family's suffering through an extra-hot summer in Toronto without successful cooling, even after seven service calls.

As for Marilovic, he spent dozens of hours preparing his case. He presented me with a thick loose-leaf binder, stuffed with documents. Preparing for small claims court is no small deal—"time-consuming, financially demanding, emotionally stressful," he said. But winning can help customers and force companies to make needed changes.

I think you should try to resolve disputes in other ways if you can. Seek mediation through government- or industry-sponsored bodies. Hire a private mediator. This can help you find your own solution and preserve your relationship with the business.

If all else fails, prepare to go to small claims court. But do not go unprepared. Get independent inspections. Bring a few witnesses. And make sure you have enough evidence to persuade a judge that you have a solid case.

INDEX